A. Morris

C000100614

Sociolinguistic Perspectives on Bilingual Educ...

Multilingual Matters

Please contact us for the latest book information:
Multilingual Matters Ltd,
Frankfurt Lodge, Clevedon Hall, Victoria Road,
Clevedon, Avon BS21 7SJ,
England

MULTILINGUAL MATTERS 84
Series Editor: Derrick Sharp

Sociolinguistic Perspectives on Bilingual Education

Christina Bratt Paulston

MULTILINGUAL MATTERS LTD
Clevedon • Philadelphia • Adelaide

Library of Congress Cataloging in Publication Data

Sociolinguistic Perspectives on Bilingual Education/Edited by Christina Bratt
Paulston
p. cm. (Multilingual Matters: 84)
Includes bibliographical references and index
1. Education, bilingual. 2. Sociolinguistics.
I. Paulston, Christina Bratt, 1932-. II. Series: Multilingual Matters (Series): 84.
LC3719.S63   1992
371.97   dc 20a

British Library Cataloguing in Publication Data

A CIP catalogue record for this book is available from the British Library.

ISBN 1-85359-147-5 (hbk)
ISBN 1-85359-146-7 (pbk)

Multilingual Matters Ltd

UK: Frankfurt Lodge, Clevedon Hall, Victoria Road, Clevedon, Avon BS21 7SJ.
USA: 1900 Frost Road, Suite 101, Bristol, PA 19007, USA.
Australia: P.O. Box 6025, 83 Gilles Street, Adelaide, SA 5000, Australia.

Copyright © 1992 Christina Bratt Paulston.

All rights reserved. No part of this work may be reproduced in any form or by
any means without permission in writing from the publisher.

Printed and bound in Great Britain by the Longdunn Press, Bristol.

Contents

Preface

These articles on bilingual education (BE) all have as a common objective trying to describe and explain bilingual education in order to predict the educational results of various policies imposed on linguistic minorities. Thus, the articles focus on theory and research rather than on the classroom perspective. The major point is that the research findings on bilingual education cannot be interpreted unless BE is interpreted as an intervening variable rather than as a causal factor. All of the articles share the viewpoint that explanatory factors of BE are to be found in the social relationship of the linguistic groups in contact, a view I am even more convinced of now than when I first proposed it in 1974.

I wrote 'Las Escuelas Bilingües' on return to the United States after two years (and two babies) in Peru. It is included here not because it was my first attempt to grapple with BE, which it was, but because it illustrates at the case study level the importance of contextual factors in interpreting BE and because it remains as accurate in that interpretation as it was when it was written.

In reading through the published research on BE, one cannot but be struck by the many disparate findings. I am sure I can find a study to support just about any possible claim. 'Ethnic Relations and Bilingual Education' is the first good paper of mine which attempts to come to terms with these contradictory findings.

Ethnic identity & assimilation and language maintenance & shift are some of the major concerns in understanding BE, and in 'Language and Ethnic Boundaries', I examine and illustrate language maintenance as a mechanism of ethnic boundary maintenance with a case study of the Swedish Sami. The paper is co-authored with my husband Rolland G. Paulston and this is an appropriate place to acknowledge his help and influence over the years.

In 'Theoretical Perspectives' I outline some major theories of social and educational change and discuss the identification and interpretation of variables of BE within the framework of each particular theory. This paper won the American Educational Research Association's Research Review Award in 1980 and it is probably one of my best.

'Biculturalism' was my TESOL presidential address and remains one of my favorite papers. I doubt that it is very popular (it is not cited very often) as it goes counter to all the facile claims of individual biculturalism. I argue that, besides surface phenomena of dress, talk, food, and behavior, individuals are not really bicultural in deep-seated values and basic world views.

'Research on BE in the United States' deals with quantitative and qualitative data on BE in terms of the relationship between theoretical paradigms and research methodology. It is an unusual topic for papers on BE research and I find it a fun paper.

In 1982 I had been asked to do a review of the (contradictory, of course) Swedish research on BE for the National Swedish Board of Education. For the conference in Stockholm where 'Problems in Comparative Analysis' was first presented, I wanted a sound and slightly boring topic because I knew it would be examined for any possible bias. (With the publication of the research review, I was of course accused of bias by those who did not like the political/pedagogical implications of the report.) This paper, which seeks to clarify problems of generalisability of BE research, was the result. It is very sound, maybe slightly boring, but it covers a topic which deserves attention, and so I have included it here.

Bilingual education is of course the result of educational language planning, so I thought that this brief paper on 'Language Planning' was a suitable conclusion to a book on sociolinguistic perspectives on bilingual education.

Sources

Chapter 1: Las Escuelas Bilingües in Perú: Some Comments on Second Language Learning. From *IRAL*, November 1972.

Chapter 2: Ethnic Relations and Bilingual Education: Accounting for Contradictory Data. From *Working Papers on Bilingualism*, No. 6, Ontario Institute for Studies in Education, May 1975.

Chapter 3: Language and Ethnic Boundaries. From *Papers from the First Nordic Conference on Bilingualism* (ed. T. Skutnabb-Kangas), Helsingfors University, 1977 (with R. G. Paulston).

Chapter 4: Theoretical Perspectives on Bilingual Education Programs. From *Working Papers on Bilingualism*, No. 13, Ontario Institute for Studies in Education, May 1977.

Chapter 5: Biculturalism: Some Reflections and Speculations. From *TESOL Quarterly*, 12 (4), 1978.

Chapter 6: Quantitative and Qualitative Research on Bilingual Education in the United States. From *Proceedings of the Third Nordic Symposium on Bilingualism*, Umeå, Sweden, 1981.

Chapter 7: Problems in the Comparative Analysis of Bilingual Education. *Scandinavian Working Papers on Bilingualism*, 1, 1982.

Chapter 8: Language Planning. From *Language Planning and Language Education* (ed. C. Kennedy), London: Allen and Unwin, 1984.

1 Las Escuelas Bilingües in Perú: Some Comments on Second Language Learning[1]

If the title of this paper would seem to promise some definitive conclusions, I want to make clear that I am reporting on the problem of the relative efficiency of bilingual education in some of its aspects and the implications for language teaching, not on any final solutions.

The Summer Institute of Linguistics runs several bilingual schools in Peru. There are two centers. One is Yarinacocha in Pucallpa, the base camp which serves some 30 Amazon jungle tribes. This is a politically sensitive area as the three bordering countries of Peru, Ecuador, and Colombia still argue the exact location of their borders. Often the Indian has not heard of either country. The other center is in Ayacucho, high in the Andes, where native bilingual teachers are trained at the University of Huamanga — by an Instituto Lingüístico professor — to teach the monolingual Quechua-speaking children in the 22 experimental schools of that *departamento*.

All the bilingual schools are part of the national public school system, but they are the only public bilingual schools in the country, and without the work of the Instituto Lingüístico there would be no schools in parts of the high windblown Sierra and lowland Amazon basin (D. Burns, 1968: 107). The Instituto is only one of a world-wide net of affiliates of the Summer Institute of Linguistics, whose basic objective is to spread the word of God, i.e. to make available Bible translations in the native tongue. Secondary objectives of the Summer Institute of Linguistics are frequently — as in Peru — to effect improvements in the areas of education, public health and community development. Instituto personnel operate in primitive areas with a high input of motivation, of resources, and of technology — such as airplanes and radio systems — not found locally.

Although the official language of Peru is Spanish, less than half of the population speak Spanish as a first language (Peru, 1966).[2] Of the Andean Indian languages, Quechua is the most common, followed by Aymara.

1

There are numerous stone-age tribes in the Amazon jungle basin, each with separate language and culture.

One cannot speak of Peruvian culture without careful modification: there are two cultures, which in turn can be separated into many subgroups and stratifications. But basically there are the minority of the superordinate Hispanic culture and the majority of the subordinate Indian, or indigenous as it is called.[3] However, Peruvians are racially mixed, or mestizo, which is to say that most are part or all Indian in origin. But race is not defined by caste as we tend to do, but rather by social class and culture (Patch, 1971), of which language is an integral part. With starched hat, braids and long wide skirts, and a community-centered world view expressed in Quechua, you are an Indian. But go to the city, cut off your hair and put on a miniskirt, and accept in Spanish a Latin egocentric world view, and you become mestizo. In fact, it is a very arduous but common process, usually taking one or two generations. Typically only the Indian and the upper class will admit knowing Quechua; for the slowly growing middle class, where you find the public school teachers and the administrators, the Indian heritage is still too uncomfortably close.

Peru's educational system is highly centralized, and all major decisions emanate from the Ministerio de Educación Pública in Lima, the heart of the Hispanic coastal area that politically, culturally, and economically replaced metropolitan Spain during the revolutionary period to internally colonize the sierra and jungle areas. The medium of instruction is Spanish, and all textbooks used to teach the national curriculum are also in Spanish. Incidentally, a commonly voiced belief is that Quechua — the language of the Incas — is too primitive a language to be written. Teachers, most often mestizos, are not likely to admit that they also understand or speak Quechua. Teachers are since 1964 relatively well paid, public education is now available to some 80% of all children, and the field of education represents an avenue of not inconsiderable upward social mobility. Although Peruvian Hispanic society is authoritative, traditional, and conservative, the culture does allow some upward social mobility as is often the case in former colonies.

In a typical rural public school in the Sierra, a Quechua child is from the first day of school taught to read, write, and count in a second language — taught by a teacher who is not likely to ever speak anything but Spanish. Not surprisingly, the school completion rates for this group are less than 10%. The jungle tribes never had any public schools until the advent of the Summer Institute of Linguistics in the 1940s, so one cannot talk of a typical school there. The Spanish-speaking children of the upper and middle classes, whose idealized culture forms the content of the public school curriculum, usually go to private schools, a situation not unlike that in many large urban areas in the United States (Paulston, 1971).

In contrast, in the bilingual schools of the Instituto Lingüístico, the *maestro,* or teacher, is always bilingual of the same tribe or region. The program calls for three years of bilingual schooling, upon the successful completion of which children enter second grade where all instruction is in Spanish. Typically, students first learn to read in their native language, which the linguist from the Instituto Lingüístico for that tribe or area has analyzed, reduced to writing, and put into primers. Concurrently the children study Spanish orally. Only after they can read well in their own language, do they begin to read in Spanish. In arithmetic, the Spanish number system is at times introduced from the beginning as some tribes have counting systems markedly different from ours. However, explanations and directions are in the native language. The teachers spend the summer vacation months of January, February and March in teacher training programs at the Instituto's centers in Ayacucho and Yarinacocha (Mendoza, 1967; Wise, n.d.).

What then is the problem that we as linguists and teachers can isolate and learn from observing? As teachers we might be most interested to know whether the bilingual schools are more 'efficient' than their monolingual counterparts. Such a simple statement of the problem leads of course to the question 'efficient at what?' or, put in another way, to a consideration of the function of public education in Peru. As teachers we are likely to interpret the problem in terms of efficient language learning — who learns Spanish better? — but it is not likely that either the policy makers in the Ministerio de Educación, who represent the Hispanic culture of Peru's ruling class, or the missionaries of the Instituto Lingüístico see the problem in those terms.

From a study of the national public school curriculum, the schools would seem to prepare an academic elite for entry into a university. In fact, it is obvious that this cannot be the case. The implicit function of the public schools has a much more important role. They are the means through which a very large and very discontented segment of the population can be brought into the mainstream of the country's life, can be acculturated into Hispanic culture with its respect for the superordinate mestizo elites. Although only some three children out of ten who begin *transición* (the first year of primary) do graduate, the vast majority of dropouts have in three or four years of schooling learned (1) the rudiments of literacy and arithmetic, (2) the inferiority of the indigenous culture *vis-à-vis* the national Hispanic culture, and (3) the impossibility of 'qualifying' for a high position because of their lack of formal education. (Paulston, 1971).

The function of education seen from the Instituto Lingüístico's viewpoint is in its simplest form to enable the people to profit from the word of God. This, they believe, can most efficiently be done in the native language (Townsend, 1966). But the Instituto Lingüístico is also concerned with the entire person — health, living conditions, and relationship to the rest of the country he or she often does not know exists. The Instituto explicitly sees the schools as a means of acculturation, although to them it is not the most important function (Solnit, 1968).

We see then that a statement of the problem as 'which type of school is most educationally efficient?' cannot be dealt with without taking into account the complex situation which led to the existence of the two types of schools.

The ministerio would consider the school most efficient which most thoroughly hispanicized the student, the Instituto would favor that school which led to the internalization of values embodied in the beliefs professed by the Instituto members, while I, the language teacher, would look for language proficiency.

Looking at the problem of the relative learning efficiency of the two types of schools, we find that it is difficult to obtain any statistically reliable data for the following reasons:

(1) The possibility of establishing any control groups in the rural jungle area is remote because of the inaccessibility of the terrain as well as the lack of resources and interest.

(2) A comparison with national norms, invalid as such a comparison would be, is not possible, since Peru does not have nationwide standardized tests.

(3) The Ministerio de Educación has shown little interest in evaluation. The Hispanic cultural attitude is not favorable to empirical research, the epistemological approach reflecting the authoritative and traditional structuring of society. It is doubtful that the Ministerio in a country where the Catholic Church is the state religion cares to give high visibility to the efforts of a Protestant missionary group in an area where the Ministerio has previously failed to establish any schools. A primary function of the schools in the jungle as perceived by the Ministerio, namely that of political socialization, is at present reasonably well fulfilled.

(4) The tribes are becoming aware of the existence of Peru and their obligations to the country, and sufficiently literate to carry out orders issued from Lima. (It was no later than the 1940s that there was a shooting war with Ecuador in this border area.) The Ministerio is not interested in any

further educational efficiency, especially in light of the impoverished and near total lack of development in the jungle.

The bilingual schools for the Quechua-speaking children of the Sierra also present many obstacles to objective evaluation. However, in 1968 there was pending a decision by the Ministerio de Educación to extend the program of the experimental schools to other parts of the Sierra with similar problems of isolated monolingual groups. This necessarily stirred an interest in evaluation, and the Instituto Lingüístico has made some attempts at comparisons with the monolingual Spanish schools in the same zone.

The director of the Instituto's Ayacucho center reports the following findings for his program (D. Burns, 1968: 108–9): Students transferred to second grade of monolingual schools before the end of their three-year bilingual schooling were capable of doing the work in reading, penmanship, nature study and civic education, moral and religious education, and language (i.e. Spanish). In some cases students placed as high as fourth and fifth grade. These conclusions were based on final examinations, December, 1967. The most difficult course for students and teachers alike is Oral Spanish. Without increased contact with the Spanish-speaking community, the students will not learn to speak fluent Spanish in the artificial surroundings of the classroom, says Dr Burns. However, the proficiency in Spanish after three years of bilingual education is definitely higher than that of students with three years of schooling in the regular school. In this instance, the conclusion is not documented. In a recent conversation, Dr Burns has also commented that absenteeism and the dropout rate are lower for the bilingual schools. In a report on education materials, Nadine Burns (1968: 4) comments: 'All students who have transferred from the bilingual schools to the common school system we have been able to follow up on are doing above average work in their schools and are changing their teachers' ideas about the effectiveness of teaching Quechua speakers in their own mother tongue.'

Although it is not possible at this point to say whether the bilingual schools are more efficient in language teaching, there are several conclusions we might draw from a study of this problem.

It cannot be said often enough that language does not exist in a vacuum, but is an integral part of a specific culture from which it cannot be separated. Language learning is not merely acquiring a new skill, but it is also learning to adapt to the culture of the language.

Speaking from personal experience, for a Swede who by necessity learns English as the *lingua franca* of Europe, the experience is not very threatening. He has a perfectly good language and culture of his own, he considers himself fully equal to anything English or American, and more importantly, he expects this to be the mutual viewpoint. But consider the learning of English by the Amerindian and the Puerto Rican. Consider the learning of French by the Moroccan, and of English by the speaker of a sub-standard dialect. The very fact that they are pressured into accepting another culture and its medium of expression is likely to seem a derogatory comment on their own culture. The point I am making is that foreign language learning and second language learning may be a much more dissimilar psychological experience than we have previously supposed it to be.[4] We need to consider more carefully the socio-psychological importance of language as the reflection of the peer group on societies which have sub- and superordinate cultures, and we need to do this in a systematic way.

There are at least two requirements for this. One is the urgent importance for the linguist and the language teacher to work closely with the other social scientists. The language teacher cannot be expected to be trained in anthropology and sociology, economics and political science. But it should be clear from considering the teaching of Spanish in Peru that the problem of the educational efficiency of the bilingual schools as compared to the monolingual schools is rendered relatively meaningless unless one understands the cultural — i.e. the social, economic, and political background — in which the schools operate. Language teachers need the various interpretations of their specific problems that the other social scientists can contribute, and it should be commonplace to say so.

The other requirement is that of evaluation research. If Burns' findings that Spanish is better taught in Quechua that in Spanish prove to be accurate, as Nancy Modiano's (1966) work in Mexico would seem to corroborate, it may well be that some of our experimental findings for foreign language learning do not hold true for second language learning. In which case, maybe we should teach English in Navajo, and Spanish in Quechua and Tzotzil, if it is language proficiency we want.

Notes

1. This article was written in 1970. I had spent two years in Peru, teaching at the Pontificia Universidad Catolica del Peru in Lima, and working as language teaching consultant with the Instituto Lingüístico. Much of the data was based on personal interviews with staff members of the Ministerio de Educación and of the Instituto Lingüístico de Verano. The issues discussed in this article remain germane, but for an update, see von Gleich (1989), Hornberger (1985) and Larson & Davis (1981).

2. The Peruvian government issued a new bilingual policy in June 1972. This policy recognizes the linguistic pluralism of the country and establishes a legal basis for the creation of bilingual schools in non-Spanish speaking areas. The government mentioned in this article refers to Peruvian governments prior to the Revolutionary Government of the Armed Forces. Although the current educational situation remains the same as described in this article, the military government's actions seem to indicate that they conceive of the school as one of the major means for bringing about social democratic reform.
3. *Indio* is since June 24, 1969 officially changed to *campesino*.
4. A second language — as opposed to a foreign language — refers to an official or semi-official language of a country, the knowledge of which is needed in order to participate in the national life, e.g., Spanish in Peru and Mexico, English in the United States and India, French in Morocco, etc.

References

BURNS, DONALD 1968, Niños de la sierra peruana estudian en quecha para saber español. *Annuario Indigenista* XXVII (December), 105–10.

BURNS, NADINE 1968. Report on education materials used in bilingual schools of Ayacucho. November (Mimeo).

HORNBERGER, N. H. 1985, Bilingual education and Quechua language maintenance in Highland Puno. Ph.D. dissertation, University of Wisconsin-Madison.

LARSON, M. L. and DAVIS, P. M. (eds) 1981, *Bilingual Education: An Experience in Peruvian Amazonia*. Washington, DC: Center for Applied Linguistics.

MENDOZA, SAMUEL P. 1967, El Instituto Lingüístico de Verano: Aglutinante Nacional, reprinted from *Revista Militar del Perú* (September–October 1966). Ministerio de Educación Pública, *Sistema de Educación Bilingüe de la Selva*. Lima, Peru.

MODIANO, NANCY D. 1966, Reading comprehension in the national language: a comparative study of bilingual and all-Spanish approaches to reading instruction in selected Indian schools in the highlands of Chiapas, Mexico. Unpublished Ph.D. dissertation, New York University.

PATCH, RICHARD W. 1971, La Parada, Lima's market: Serrano and Criollo, the confusion of race with class. *AUFSR*, West Coast South American Series, XIV, No. 2 (February).

PAULSTON, ROLLAND G. 1971, *Society, Schools and Progress in Peru*. Oxford: Pergamon Press.

Peru 1966, *VI Censo Nacional de Población: 1966. Idiomas, Alfabetismo, Asistencia Escolar, Nivel de Educación*, Vol. III.

SOLNIT, ALBERT J. 1968, *Bilingual Education and Community Development*. Lima: Summer Instituto of Linguistics and Ministry of Public Education.

TOWNSEND, WILLIAM C. 1966, founder of the Summer Institute of Linguistics, as quoted by Samuel Mendoza in 'El Instituto Lingüístico de Verano,' reprinted from *Revista Militar del Perú* (September–October), 5.

VON GLEICH, U. 1989, *Educación Primaria Bilingüe Intercultural en América Latina*. Rossdorf, Germany: Deutsche Gesellschaft für Technische Zusammenarbeit.

WISE, MARY RUTH n.d., Utilizing languages of minority groups in a bilingual experiment in the Amazonian jungle of Peru. Summer Institute of Linguistics, Yarinacocha, Peru (Mimeo).

2 Ethnic Relations and Bilingual Education: Accounting for Contradictory Data

I have been invited to review some of the 'hard data' on bilingual education and discuss some of the questions raised thereby regarding the efficacy of bilingual education (particularized to different models if possible).

I should make clear from the outset my particular bias when it comes to 'hard data'. I consider as hard data any systematic and sustained observation within a coherent theoretical framework. I am impressed with the technical degree of sophistication of much psychometric research but find many of the findings inadequate in scope to deal with the questions and problems of bilingual education. It is simply *not* so that we can understand only what we can measure, and I doubt that we will ever be able to reduce the most important issues in bilingual education to quantifiable terms. My bias, then, is primarily that of a social anthropologist like Pelto (1970): 'I put strong emphasis on quantification and statistics, but I feel strongly that many of the more qualitative aspects of anthropological working styles are essential to effective research.' It is within such a framework that I will attempt to interpret the research findings on bilingual education.

I have restricted the following discussion to bilingualism only as it occurs within an educational setting, and have thus excluded the large body of literature on language acquisition as it occurs in a natural setting. In limiting this paper, I have chosen (1) to bring together some data on bilingual education on which there is both consensus and disagreement, (2) to summarize some theoretical frameworks for interpreting the data, and (3) to try to account for the apparent contradictory findings.

The major viewpoint from which this paper is written is that we can begin to understand the problems and questions of bilingual education *only when we see bilingual education as the result of certain societal factors rather than as the cause of certain behaviors in children.* Virtually all the research on bilingual education treats the bilingual education programs as the independent or causal variable, as the factor which accounts for certain subsequent results. A case in point is the vast number of studies which have attempted to assess students' reading achievements by standardized test scores where the independent variable, or the 'treatment' as it is occasionally referred to, is the language (mother tongue or L2) used as medium of instruction. I know of no experimental study on reading achievement which looks at language medium of instruction as an intervening or dependent variable, i.e. as a variable which is either a factor modifying the effects of the independent variable, or which is the result of certain conditions. Verdoodt's (1972) study is an example of the kind of research I have in mind — an attempt to explain variation of phenomena in language maintenance and shift within consistent theoretical frameworks.

One of the difficulties with research that looks at the bilingual program or school as the independent variable (like the Canadian immersion programs and Mackey's J. F. Kennedy school in Berlin), is that such studies carry in and by themselves virtually no generalizability to other programs, as Mackey (1972) is careful to point out.

Such case studies, however, are necessary, if we are to begin to develop a theory of bilingual education which will enable us to generalize the evidence from the individual studies and to account for their often contradictory findings. It is my contention that we can best do so within a framework of comparative ethnic relations and revitalization theory. Without question, there are other theoretical approaches possible, but it is very clear to me that unless we try in some way to account for the socio-historical, cultural, and economic-political factors which lead to certain forms of bilingual education, we will never understand the consequences of that education. In other words, we need research which looks at bilingual education as the intervening or dependent variable, and we don't have it.

Before looking at the actual research, I would like to cite some crucial distinctions which Gaarder (n.d.) makes about bilingualism. He distinguishes between elitist bilingualism and folk bilingualism. Elitist bilingualism, he points out, is the hallmark of intellectuals and the learned in most societies, and, one might add, of upper-class membership in many societies such as in continental Europe. It is a matter of choice. Not so with folk bilingualism which is the result of ethnic groups in contact and competition within a single state, where one of the peoples becomes bilingual involuntarily in order to survive.

As I have pointed out in an earlier paper (C. B. Paulston, 1975), the research findings are quite clear on one point. Upper- and middle-class children do perfectly well whether they are schooled in the mother tongue or in the L2, although we don't really know why. Elitist bilingual education has never been an educational problem, and therefore this paper will deal with folk bilingual education — a result of ethnic groups in contact and competition.

There are three basic types of bilingual education:

(1) *Immersion* programs where all schooling is in the L2, with the possible exception of a component in the mother tongue skills. The L2 is typically an official language, although exceptions exist with immersion programs in a language of wider communication than the official language (all elitist bilingual education programs are also of this latter type).

(2) Programs taught in the *mother tongue* with an SL component, i.e. the target language is usually an official language or a language of wider communication (or both).

(3) Programs in which *two languages* are used as the medium of instruction. Various models exist. The majority of this type of bilingual education that I am familiar with involves the use of an official language and a minority language.

This paper primarily examines the issues raised in situations where children study in a language other than their mother tongue, the situation in which the issues I want to discuss are most clearly delineated.

Bilingual Programs

'Immersion' or 'home–school language switch' programs are the terms by which the Canadian programs have become known. All beginning instruction is given in French to anglophone students, and the school language is different from the home language. Actually, this is a very common form of schooling in many parts of the world, and one which has given rise to world-wide debate of the issues involved. Since Patricia Engle (1973) and I (C. B. Paulston, 1975) have outlined and discussed some of these issues before, I will barely touch upon them here. Reduced to the basic issues, the argument concerns: (1) the *choice of medium of instruction,* whether in the mother tongue or the L2, and consequent achievement of language skills, especially in initial reading; (2) the *achievement of subject matter knowledge* in fields like math, science, etc. in the mother tongue compared to in the L2; and (3) the *concern about possible deleterious cognitive effects* of following a curriculum in a second language. Engle, after reviewing 25 studies, could only report that 'none has as yet conclusively answered the question posed in the initial paragraph [i.e. the first two issues above]'. In an attempt to account for the discrepancy of various findings, I will cite three North American studies of immersion programs. They are the Chiapas (Modiano, 1966, 1973), the St Lambert (Lambert & Tucker, 1972), and the Culver City (Campbell, 1970, 1972a, 1972b) studies.

In the Chiapas, Mexico study, Modiano found that Indian children who had received initial reading in the vernacular and then in Spanish scored higher on tests of reading comprehension after three years than those who had been taught only in Spanish. There are other studies which support her findings.

The St Lambert findings, however, clearly contradict them. The St Lambert program is the prototype of the recent Canadian immersion programs where anglophone children enter programs where they are initially taught only in French with components taught in the later grades in the mother tongue. In the St Lambert study, kindergarten and first grade children were taught exclusively in French with the addition of an English period in second grade. By the end of that grade, the students were reading equally well as the English controls, were also able to read in French, and they maintained this achievement through the other grades. Further, the success of the Canadian immersion programs can be measured not only by the battery of standardized tests with which they are being carefully assessed but also by their proliferation and popularity. Swain & Barik (1978) report that 'currently some 40 percent of English-speaking children in the Montreal area enter French immersion kindergarten classes'.

The Culver City, California program is a carefully evaluated replication of the St Lambert experiment. English-speaking children are taught only in Spanish from kindergarten on with a later component of English language skills; according to Cohen & Lebach (1973), it is the only Spanish immersion program in public education in the United States. The assessment findings are similar to those of St Lambert. At the end of grade two, there are no signs of retardation in English language skills, oral or reading. In Spanish reading, they did not do as well as a comparison group in Quito, Ecuador, but as well as their native Spanish-speaking classmates, and when compared to native Spanish-speaking students in California taking the *Prueba de Lectura Nivel 1*, they were at the 90th percentile in the total reading score. In mathematics they scored higher than the English comparison group.

There is, however, one aspect of the program which differs from the Canadian immersion programs. Although all immediately involved in the program — students, parents and teachers — expressed satisfaction with it, 'a major controversy broke out whether the Spanish-only kindergarten program could continue' (Cohen, 1974: 95–103). Cohen reports:

> At a Culver City board meeting, a parent in the Culver City community publicly read a section of the Education Code of the State of California (Section 71), which requires that the basic language of instruction in all schools in the State be English, and that only after a child becomes fluent in a foreign language can he be instructed in that language. . . . Willing to test the matter in court, if necessary, the Culver City school board voted to initiate a second Immersion kindergarten class. At its January 1972 meeting, the California State Board of Education unanimously approved the Culver City decision to establish a new *Spanish-only* kindergarten class. (Cohen, 1974: 95–103)

There has been no similar controversy involved with the Canadian programs; on the contrary, the Canadian programs have been initiated by parents' concern and continued support.

At this point, I would like to pose two questions. The first is: why is it that we have no conclusive answer to such a seemingly simple question as, 'Will a child learn to read more rapidly in his second language if he is first taught to read in his primary language?' (Engle, 1973: 63). The answer, I think, is clear. It is true that differences in research designs of the various studies will have influenced the findings, but even so there ought to be some discernible trends, but there are not. It is simply that medium of instruction in school programs is an intervening variable rather than the causal variable, as it is always treated in all these studies on reading achievement by children from ethnic groups and languages in contact. By merely examining intervening variables, one cannot hope to achieve any similarity and consensus in the research findings, as indeed we don't have.

The next question is obvious: How can we account for the contradictory consequences of similar programs in Mexico, Canada, and California? In my earlier paper (C. B. Paulston, 1975: 38–9), I pointed out that 'social class of the students was the one overruling factor. In every single study where monolingual children did as well as or better in L2 instruction than did native speakers, those children came from upper- or middle-class homes'. Although I have not really seen any evidence to convince me otherwise, the trouble with that statement is that it does not explain very much. True, it indicates another causal variable for school achievement of children, but it has limited explanatory power. It does at least provide an alternative interpretation of the different research findings of the Chiapas lower-class children and the St Lambert and Culver City middle-class children. But it does not account for the 'raging' (Cohen's term) controversy of the Culver City program. It is likely that social class membership is itself an intervening variable, and that we must 'tease apart' that concept.

For that purpose I turn to Schermerhorn's (1970) 'inductive typology' as he has outlined it in *Comparative Ethnic Relations: A Framework for Theory and Research*. The problems we are concerned with here — the consequences of bilingual education — are the direct result of ethnic groups in contact. Says Schermerhorn (1970: 68) 'The probability is overwhelming that when two groups with different cultural histories establish contacts that are regular rather than occasional or intermittent, one of the two groups will typically assume dominance over the other', and he says elsewhere it is the nature of this dominance which is the major factor in ethnic relations. The central question then in comparative research in ethnic relations (exactly what we are attempting to do at a low level) is 'What are the conditions that foster or prevent the integration of ethnic groups into their environing societies' (Schermerhorn, 1970: 14). (Language maintenance and language shift are concomitant conditions of the degree of integration.) He goes on to say that the task of intergroup research is to account for the modes of integration (and conflict) as dependent variables in the relations between dominant groups and subordinate ethnic groups in different societies. He then offers a skeleton outline of the central issues in such research:

> We begin with the proposition that when the territory of a contemporary nation-state is occupied by peoples of diverse cultures and origins, the integration of such plural groups into each environing society will be a composite function of three independent and three intervening variables. The independent variables posited here are: 1) repeatable sequences of interaction between subordinate ethnics and dominant groups, such as annexation, migration, and colonization; 2) the degree of enclosure (institutional separation or segmentation) of the subordinate group or groups from the society-wide network of institutions and associations; and 3) the degree of control exercised by dominant groups over access to scarce resources by subordinate groups in a given society.

> The intervening or contextual variables that modify the effects of independent variables are: 1) agreement or disagreement between dominant and subordinate groups on collective goals for the latter, such as assimilation, pluralism; 2) membership of a society under scrutiny in a class or category of societies sharing overall common cultural and structural features, such as Near-East societies, Sub-Saharan African societies; 3) membership of a society under scrutiny in a more limited category of societies distinguished by forms of institutional

dominance, i.e. polity dominating economy or vice versa. (Schermer-horn, 1970: 15)

Let us now look at our three studies in the light of this theoretical frame-work. In French-speaking Canada, the ethnic groups came into contact through voluntary migration, the subtype of intergroup sequences which involve the least coercive control. In Canada, the English later took over by force, and this presumably is reflected in the degree of enclosure. By degree of enclosure, Schermerhorn refers to a social or structural pluralism which varies from maximum to minimal forms which can be conceptualized as degrees of enclosure with indicators like endogamy and institutional dupli-cation. In other words, the more the two groups share social institutions like the same churches, the same schools, the same jobs, the less the degree of enclosure within that society. The persistent maintenance of two languages within one province is indicative of the existence of a structual pluralism in Quebec, of institutional differences which separate the ethnic groups in terms of social participation. This structural pluralism is also one of the causes of the immersion programs because it is the lack of contact between English- and French-speaking peer groups which have necessitated them. One need only look at a multilingual city like Tangier to see how effortlessly children become bi/trilingual in contact situations.

Schermerhorn's third independent variable, the degree of control by the dominant group, raises some of the most interesting issues of the Cana-dian immersion programs. Widespread individual bilingualism of two offi-cial languages leads typically to the disappearance of one of the languages or to a diglossic situation, and as Gaarder believes, balanced folk bilingualism simply is not a feasible situation. It is typically the subordinate group which becomes bilingual with resultant language shift over two or three genera-tions. This has been the situation in French-speaking Canada until now, where there has been a steady shift to English, which is the dominant language of business and industry. Until recently, the size of the French-speaking population has remained steady in spite of the number of French speakers who shifted to English — a function of structural pluralism, i.e. different religious institutions with different ideologies such as the Canadian Roman Catholic opposition to birth control.

In societies where ethnic groups — who have sufficient power to enforce it — want to maintain their language, they typically take legal mea-sures to protect their language. This is what happened in Belgium, where bilingual education was outlawed, and it is happening in Canada. In 1967, French and English were declared to be official languages of Canada. At present, there are pressure groups which are urging the Quebec provincial government not only to preserve but to strengthen the position of the French language. As Swain (1974: 2) summarizes:

(1) The French-Canadians are making serious attempts to maintain their native language and culture. For the present, this appears to imply a concomitant move towards French unilingualism.

(2) The English-Canadians, threatened neither by native language loss nor by cultural assimilation, and gradually accepting possible economic and educational advantages to the learning of French, are manifesting an increased interest in acquiring bilingual skills. (Swain, 1974: 2)

In other words, we have the unusual situation where the economically dominant group is becoming bilingual, thereto motivated by economic concerns for the future brought about by legal measures and pressures by the other group in political power.

Now let us look at the intervening variables. In order to deal with the agreement or disagreement between dominant and subordinate groups on collective goals for the latter, such as assimilation or pluralism, Schermerhorn (1970: 85) sets up a paradigm of which one purpose is to 'specify the social contexts that can serve as intervening variables in answer to the scientific query, "under what conditions?"' He bases his discussion on Wirth's typology of the different policies adopted by minority groups in response to their clearly unprivileged position:

These policies he called assimilationist, pluralist, secessionist, and militant. Briefly, assimilationist policy seeks to merge the minority members into the wider society by abandoning their own cultural distinctiveness and adopting their superordinates' values and style of life. The pluralist strategy solicits tolerance from the dominant group that will allow the subordinates to retain much of their cultural distinctiveness. The secessionist minority aims to separate or detach itself from the superordinates so as to pursue an independent existence. Finally, the militants . . . intend to gain control over the dominants who currently have the ascendency. (Schermerhorn, 1970: 78)

Schermerhorn points out that assimilation and pluralism really refer to cultural aspects while secession and militancy refer to structural.

To clarify this problem it is well to insist on the analytic distinction between culture and social structure. Culture signifies the ways of action learned through socialization, based on norms and values that serve as guides or standards for that behaviour. Social structure, on the other hand, refers to the set of crystallized social relationships which its

> (the society's) members have with each other which places them in groups, large or small, permanent or temporary, formally organized or unorganized, and which relates them to the major institutional activities of the society, such as economic and occupational life, religion, marriage and the family, education, government, and recreation. (Schermerhorn, 1970: 81)

In order to deal with the difficulty of applying cultural features to conditions which involve social features, he (Schermerhorn, 1970: 81) suggests the paired concepts of centripetal and centrifugal trends in social life. 'Centripetal tendencies refer both to cultural trends such as acceptance of common values, styles of life, etc., as well as structural features like increased participation in a common set of groups, associations, and institutions.' To keep the two aspects distinct, he calls the first assimilation, the latter incorporation. Much has been written about bilingual education and assimilation, and I think it would very much clarify our own thinking if we were careful to distinguish between assimilation and incorporation. Many subordinate groups in the United States do not want to abandon their cultural distinctiveness; rather what they want is access to goods and services, to the institutional privileges held by the English-speaking middle class, i.e. economic incorporation rather than assimilation. (The legislative measures taken in regard to French can also be seen as a way of regulating language use as a means of access to institutional privileges and promptly recognized as such by the English-speaking parents.)

> Centrifugal tendencies among subordinate groups are those that foster separation from the dominant group or from societal bonds in one respect or another. Culturally this most frequently means retention and preservation of the group's distinctive traditions in spheres like language, religion, recreation, etc., together with the particularistic values associated with them: Wirth's cultural pluralism. But in order to protect these values, structural requirements are needed, so there are demands for endogamy, separate associations, and even at times a restricted range of occupations. (Schermerhorn, 1970: 81–2)

Schermerhorn's major point is that integration, which involves the satisfaction of the ethnic group's modal tendency, whether it be centripetal or centrifugal, depends on the agreement or congruence of views by the dominant and subordinate groups on the goals of the latter.

If we restrict our discussion about the Canadian immersion programs to the province of Quebec, it seems that the relationship between the two ethnic groups is best symbolized by Cell B of the chart in Figure 2.1.

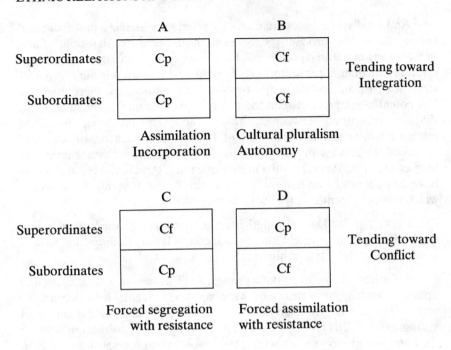

Cp = Centripetal trends
Cf = Centrifugal trends

Source: Schermerhorn, 1970: 83

FIGURE 2.1   *Congruent and incongruent orientations toward centripetal and centrifugal trends of subordinates as viewed by themselves and superordinates*

As I mentioned before, there is no clear sub/superordinate status between the two groups: the English-speaking Canadians are dominant in the economic sphere, while the government 'is solidly in the hands of the French' (Lieberson, 1970: 2). The French-speaking population want sufficient autonomy and separateness to preserve their own language and customs, like their counterpart in Switzerland whom Schermerhorn cites as an example. The English-speaking Canadians, who have actually little choice in the matter, are content to tolerate the cultural and structural pluralism of the French. 'Since both sides agree on a limited separation (live and let live — a centrifugal tendency) this represents another form of integration — looser and at least partly disengaged' (Schermerhorn, 1970: 84).

And finally, the two ethnic groups belong to the same multi-national sector, that of Western Europe. Schermerhorn postulates that policies and practices toward ethnic groups will have more comparable outcomes in any given sector than other sectors. One might add that sharing similarities of structural institutions, the major basis of the classification, there might be less potential conflict between the two groups. One might conclude, then, that the basic trend between the two ethnic groups in Canada is toward integration in Schermerhorn's sense of the term, and on such basis we could postulate the success of bilingual education programs for either group, as long as such programs remain a matter of choice. And social class, it seems to me, might not be an issue, since I can see no factor within the situation which serves to identify it (*per se*) as a variable.

I have digressed at such length in order to introduce a theoretical framework within which we might intepret our contradictory findings. Let us now briefly look at the relationship of ethnic groups in Culver City.

In California, the two ethnic groups, English-speaking Americans and Spanish-speaking Americans of Mexican origin, came into contact by annexation, an intergroup sequence which modally results in the condition symbolized by Cell D in Figure 2.1. It is characterized by a situation in which the dominant group sees the goal of the subordinate group as one of assimilation while the subordinate group shows strong centrifugal trends, in other words a situation which tends toward conflict.

Schermerhorn (1970: 124) points out that we do not have a very clear idea of the degree of enclosure of plural societies which are the result of annexation. In plural societies, 'institutions of kinship, religion, the economy, education, recreation and the like are parallel but different in structure and norms. Ordinarily, this is compounded by differences in language and sometimes by race as well.' We may not know the exact degree of enclosure, but certainly the condition exists in the United States' Southwest. Schermerhorn adds, that since language has been the most salient distinguishing mark of the plural constituents, this has given cultural features the most prominent place instead of structural characteristics. If I interpret him correctly, we have tended to understand the relationship between ethnic groups (such as in California) in terms of cultural features, but a more accurate understanding would follow if we included an examination of the structural characteristics of the relationship, especially as they express the power relation between the two groups.

'The higher the degree of enclosure of the ethnic group coupled with a high degree of control over its scarce rewards by a dominant group, the greater the conflict' (Schermerhorn, 1970: 135). I don't know how to estimate the degree of control Anglos hold over Mexican Americans, but the Chicano's perception of the power relationship between the two groups may be used as an indicator.

In interpreting the significance of the Culver City study, one should keep in mind that it is a program for the dominant group, that its native Spanish-speaking students are not members of the subordinate group, but are Latin American middle-class students, and that it was initiated, not by the parents as in the Canadian case, but from above as it were. That it is a unique program is significant; we have seen the proliferation of immersion programs in Canada, but in California there are no socio-structural incentives for parents to want their children to become bilingual. Were Spanish to become an official language by law in California, the situation no doubt would change. The Culver City program demonstrates what *can* be done with idealism and dedication in a bilingual education program. I also think the difference between the identical St Lambert and Culver City programs, the presence of conflict, and the lack of request for similar programs by interested parent groups demonstrates that bilingual education programs are the result of social factors. There is no question that children can become bilingual through education programs, but will they?

This is one of the major problems in Latin America in teaching Spanish to the indigenous ethnic groups, where the debate on how to produce bilingual schoolchildren has primarily centered around whether children should learn to read in the vernacular or in Spanish — the official language. The Chiapas study exemplifies this situation.

In order to understand the issues of bilingual education in Latin America, the relationship of ethnic groups in Mexico deserves a brief consideration. The ethnic groups came into contact through colonization:

> The colonial section in Mexico almost completely destroyed the cultural and social autonomy of the Indians, not only by liquidating the leaders but by transporting Indians to *encomiendas* and towns, where they were incorporated as laborers in a new economy, by miscegenation, and by converting them to a different religion which integrated them more fully into a unitary whole with their conquerors. (Schermerhorn, 1970: 149)

For various reasons, racism took a very mild form in Mexico, and race came to be defined largely by language, dress, and worldview, rather than by genetic characteristics. The degree of enclosure that American blacks were subjected to rarely, if ever, occurred in Mexico, and the assimilation of Indians into the Blanco group (i.e. *arribismo*) was and is a continuing process and possibility. This cholofication process is not easy and is often stretched out over several generations, invariably accompanied by language shift. It is the third independent variable which is the important one, the control of access to scarce rewards which is in all of Latin America (except Cuba) almost complete. As Heath's (1972) study of language policy in Mexico since the colonial days makes quite clear, whenever jobs which required a knowledge of Spanish were available to the Indians, they would learn Spanish. Without access to rewards, Spanish was not and is not salient.

As far as agreement on the collective goals for the indigenous ethnic groups, there is generally complete agreement of *castellanización,* and the only conflict that is likely to occur from the school program comes not from teaching reading in Spanish but in the vernacular which the parents object to as they say the children already know their mother tongue. The purpose of school from the indigenous parents' viewpoint is to teach the rudiments of Spanish and arithmetic.

Why, then, should the children in the Chiapas study have learned to read better in their mother tongue? The first reason, I think, is a linguistic one. No one has really claimed that it is not easier and faster to teach children to read in their mother tongue; the immersion studies data are quite clear on that point, and it takes the immersion children three years of schooling to catch up with the mother tongue readers. The point here is that children *can* learn to read in an L2 and that they eventually will catch up.

The second reason, I think, concerns the quality of the school program. The lack of control by the ethnic groups over access to goods and services inevitably results in less of a quality education program than those reserved for the children of the dominant group. It makes little sense to compare the results of two prestige programs in two of the richest nations of the world with a hinterland program whose teachers had a sixth-grade education. Unless L2 programs are of excellent quality and give recognition to the fact that they are teaching in a second language, children will learn better in their mother tongue. The experiment with Hiligaynon-speaking children who were taught in experimental classes with Hiligaynon, Tagalog and in English as the medium of instruction supports this view. (Ramos, Aguilar & Sibayan, 1967). The literacy rate of the children was higher in Tagalog and in English than in their mother tongue, and Aguilar interprets this as due to modern teaching and well written materials. The success of the New Primary Approach in Kenya, which involved changing from the vernaculars to English, was also due primarily to the quality of the program. In commenting on the reasons for its success, Prator (1966: 27) mentions: 'It provided much more adequate texts and teaching materials than had ever before been

available and it was carried out under almost ideal conditions of close supervision and continuous in-service training of teachers.' 'The mid-way report
on the sixth-year primary project' (Institute of Education, n.d.) of the University of Ife, Western Nigeria, comments on the perennial difficulties of
teaching English (an official language in Nigeria); the remark is equally valid
for the teaching of a second, official language in many parts of the world:

> It is well known that the two major problems in teaching English are
> teachers and books, which qualitatively and quantitatively, are usually
> in inadequate supply. The problem of teachers is by far the greater and
> more serious. Whereas inadequate books in the hands of adequate
> teachers could still produce effective and efficient learning on the part
> of pupils, even the most adequate books in the hands of inadequate
> teachers are practically useless. (Institute of Education, n.d.: 12)

It would be tempting at this point to write off all differences in children's
school achievement to the quality of the educational program. But we cannot do so. I have reported before on Ramirez' (n.d.) observation on the rate
of achievement of mother tongue literacy by the children in his La Mar
Center bilingual program. These students, children of migrant Chicano farm
workers in Texas, learned to read at a rate 75% slower than the middle-
upper-class students in a Mexico City kindergarten for whom the material in
the reading program was originally designed. The degree of excellence of a
program is not sufficient to account for the scholastic achievement of children from subordinate groups who are denied access to national rewards.

Children learn much more than language skills in school. The mid-way
report recognizes this:

> Indeed, he [the child] is completely alienated from his agricultural
> background and can only see himself generally as a failure, a person
> doomed to be the cutter of the grass on the lawn, the hewer of wood
> and the drawer of water for those few friends of his who will have the
> fortune of continuing their formal education. (Institute of Education,
> n.d.: 6)

Rolland G. Paulston (1971), in a study of social and educational stratification has commented on a number of latent educational functions in Peru:

> Thus, schooling both facilitates limited upward mobility, reinforces
> existing class divisions, and provides a means by which the masses of
> cholo children learn an idealized version of the reward of national His-
> panic culture. Even the vast majority of cholo children who drop out
> learn the rudiments of literacy and arithmetic, the inferiority of their
> cholo status and Indian origin and the superiority of the superordinate

groups who enjoy rewards 'appropriate' to their high status. Public school children are in short taught 'their place.' (R. G. Paulston, 1971: 413)

In interpreting the results of the Chiapas study, one must keep in mind the teacher variable, as indeed Modiano does. The children in the Spanish medium schools learned more from the two Indian teachers than from the mestizos, although less than the children who studied in the vernacular. The influence of teachers who come from the same culture and ethnic group as the children on children's school achievement and perception of self certainly merits careful investigation, and Engle (1973) is very right when she points out how infrequently the variable of the teacher is studied.

To sum up the Chiapas study, there is little doubt that in school programs of dubious quality where one function of education is 'to convince the stigmatized that the stigma is deserved,' (Hymes, 1971: 3) education in the vernacular seems to be more efficient than in the L2. This is probably due to psychological as well as linguistic factors, and the degree of influence native teachers have on language achievement is not clear. One would wish for a study which compared a Spanish program and a vernacular program along Modiano's design, to a program with a component of systematic presentation of oral Spanish and reading in Spanish but in which the teacher and the students freely used the vernacular. My guess is that after three years, the students in the latter group would do as well in reading as the vernacular group. A predictable difficulty lies with the teachers; in a culture which defines race by language, it is difficult to keep bilingual teachers from identifying with the mestizo rather than with the indigenous ethnic group, as indeed Heath's (1972) study documents. And such an alternative program would have to be considered very carefully in light of the Swedish data I will introduce later.

At this point, it strikes me as useful to follow Schermerhorn's comparative ethnic relations approach, and to look at ethnic groups in contact and their schooling in situations similar to those we discussed earlier. I have chosen the case of ethnic minorities in Sweden, for several reasons: (1) the situations of the Saami and the Finnish-speaking Swedes parallel the situation of the Mexican Indians and the Mexican Americans; (2) there exist a multitude of studies with hard data, which since they are written in Swedish are not very accessible and I thought it might be helpful to make them so; and (3) Sweden is a quasi-socialist country where problems of health care, diet, and unemployment are not intervening variables. Such conditions are occasionally cited as contributory factors in the lack of school achievement by children of subordinated groups.

Although I cannot, in any detail, go into the case of the reindeer-herding Saami, one point should be made in passing. Schermerhorn's theoretical framework works very well for a society in equilibrium, but typically many ethnic groups go through a revolutionary phase, a militant strategy as in Wirth's typology. In order to best understand the change of priorities in education and the various forms bilingual education takes, I find Anthony Wallace's (1966) schema of revitalization movements the most elucidating.

The situation of the Saami is similar to that of the Mexican Indians in all but one aspect. They share the sequence of colonization, the same enclosure by geographical distance if not by social institutions, virtually the same degree of control first by the church and later by the government. But the reindeer-herding Saami share the Navajo's strong disagreement with the government on their collective goal of assimilation into Swedish, respectively United States culture and society, and this disagreement becomes reflected in their education programs.

Wallace (1966: 38–9) has suggested the term revitalization movement for 'deliberate, organized conscious efforts by members of a society to construct a more satisfying culture'. A group of society involved in a revitalization movement undergoes a revolutionary phase. Says Wallace:

> But for our purposes three contrasting value orientations (for determining what is to be learnt) are most significant: the revolutionary, or utopian, orientation; the conservative . . . orientation; and the reactionary orientation. What a man is expected to do in his life will, in part, depend on whether he lives in a revolutionary, conservative, or reactionary society.

He outlines the priorities of learning in the model in Figure 2.2.

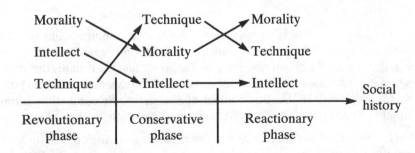

Source: Wallace (1966: 34)

FIGURE 2.2 *Learning priorities in revolutionary, conservative, and reactionary societies*

Groups undergoing a revolutionary phase will always stress moral learning, and conflicts are certain to arise when a revitalization movement takes place within a conservative society where technique has the highest learning priority, i.e. 'in conservative societies, schools prepare people not for sacrifice but for jobs' (R. G. Paulston, 1972: 478). Language skills in the official language must be seen as an aspect of technique, an aspect of preparation for jobs. The mother tongue, on the other hand, is an aspect of moral learning, reaffirming the solidarity and cultural uniqueness of the ethnic group, underscoring the need to teach the moral values of good and evil, right and wrong, the values of the old gods, in the language in which those values were originally transmitted. Reaffirmation of cultural values is frequently a part of the moral teaching, especially among ethnic groups who, prior to the revitalization movement, have been taught by the dominant group to have nothing but contempt for their own culture. The conflict over learning priorities explains the extreme importance of control over local educational institutions. I have frequently heard my colleagues comment that the best bilingual schools are those that are under community control — be it Navajo or Chicano. I am not certain what 'best' means in this connection. In my discussion of the Erickson (1969) report in my earlier paper (C. B. Paulston, 1975), I pointed out that rhetoric about cultural pluralism accounts for little if the objectives are not implemented; the community run Navajo school, as measured by the achievement test batteries from the California Test Bureau, was markedly inferior academically to the government run school. I was at the time interested only in investigating the learning of English language skills, but even so that statement — and the evaluation itself — shows our typical tendency to assess and evaluate the schooling of groups undergoing a revitalization movement with moral learning as the priority in terms of the standards of the conservative society — the standards of technique.

One aspect of 'best' is very clear. Without community control, the ethnic group will not be able to implement its learning priorities. This has been the case of the Saami who have had to go outside the formal education system to form their own institution, the Jokkmokk Folk High School (R. G. Paulston, 1974). But control of the early schooling of children remains a crucial need for the success of a revitalization movement.

I realize the total inadequacy of the preceding discussion; the topic of revitalization movements must be pursued at length if we are to understand (1) those exceptional (but characterized by a uniform process) cases where the acquisition of jobs no longer holds first priority within the social group, and (2) the consequences for bilingual education and its results.

The last situation of ethnic groups in contact I want to examine is that of the Finnish-speaking Swedes in Tornedalen in Northern Sweden. Their situation is in many aspects similar to the Chicanos'. They came into contact with the Swedes by annexation and, as is typical in such situations, their access to economic rewards was limited compared to the Swedes — the majority of them are members of Social Group 3, the Swedish euphemism for lower class (Jaakkola, 1973). But there is one important difference: the Finns totally agreed with the Swedes on the collective goals for the former — rapid and total assimilation. This is an unusual situation, symbolized by Cell A in Figure 2.1, to accompany annexation, as Schermerhorn points out. I would speculate that the situation was brought about by the lack of enclosure of social institutions and the access to and availability of jobs, most of which necessitated some knowledge of Swedish. The situation exemplifies Brudner's (1973) thesis, jobs select language learning strategies.

On the basis of these facts, we could predict integration and concomitant language learning. It is exactly what we find: integration (with indicators like name changes to Swedish, intermarriage, migration to southern Sweden, etc.) and massive language shift by a willing Finnish-speaking population. The integration was apparently not hindered by the ruthless assimilation policy carried out by the Swedes. The existence of a language problem in the schools was denied by the administration, the use of Finnish was forbidden by law in the classroom, even to monolingual Finnish-speaking children. The children were punished by the withdrawal of food for speaking Finnish in the classroom and even on the sports grounds, where one could see the strange sight of a soccer team communicating by sign language (Tenerz, 1966). Substitute Indian or Chicano for Tornedaling, and you have read it all before.

With peaceful and massive integration, one would expect that the school achievement of these children had been a successful and contributing factor. Instead we find massive school failure and early dropouts, a dismal situation which has led to a heated debate about *dubbel halvspråkighet*.

The concept of *double semilingualism* was apparently introduced earlier (Ringbom, 1962) but was brought to general recognition by Nils E. Hansegård (1968) in his work (and I translate the title) *Bilingualism or Semilingualism?* By semilingualism is meant, and I translate from Loman's (1974b: 43) summary:

> Semilingualism has been used as a term for the type of 'faulty linguistic competence' which has especially been observed in individuals who have since childhood had contact with two languages without sufficient or adequate training and stimulation in either of the two languages.

> The intellectual as well as the emotional consequences of semi-lingualism have been pointed out. Semilingualism makes the individual's communication with others more difficult and even leads to a repression of the emotional life; speech becomes inhibited and without spontaneity. (Loman, 1974b: 43)

In other words, by knowing two languages poorly, the children know no language well and this condition has negative emotional, psychological, cognitive, linguistic, and scholastic consequences. I must admit that the first time I was exposed to the notion of semilingualism, I dismissed it out of hand as utter nonsense. Anyone trained in the tradition of structural linguistics knows very well that any language is perfectly adequate for the needs of its speakers. Or so I thought. I subsequently came across an article by Bloomfield (1964: 395) himself which contains in passing this touching description of White-Thunder:

> White-Thunder, a man round forty, speaks less English than Menomini, and that is a strong indictment, for his Menomini is atrocious. His vocabulary is small, his inflections are often barbarous, he constructs sentences of a few threadbare models. He may be said to speak no language tolerably. His case is not uncommon among younger men, even when they speak but little English. Perhaps it is due, in some indirect way, to the impact of the conquering language. (Bloomfield, 1964: 395)

And that set me reconsidering the matter of semilingualism. I still do not know what to think, except that we need to consider the problem with open minds.

The major point that Hansegård and Tenerz — the two major proponents for recognition of the widespread existence of double semilingualism — make is that children must become literate in the mother tongue in order to counteract the negative effects of double semilingualism. Although both take the approach of cultural pluralism, one of the major goals of the school curriculum which they outline is increased language skills in Swedish. One factor in evaluating their claims cannot be ignored; both men have had extensive classroom experience with the children they describe and the present school system they criticize. It is difficult to dismiss as inaccurate and irrelevant years of first-hand contact and observation of their own students.

Let us now look at some data which addresses itself to the possibility of existence of semilingualism.

A study by Henrysson & Ljung (1967), which controlled for social class and intelligence, found that in the sixth grade, the bilingual students did considerably worse than the monolingual Swedish-speaking children in Swedish and English, the subjects tested.

Jaakkola (1974) concludes in a study that the bilingual subjects did worse in both a Swedish and a Finnish synonym test than did those who had either language as dominant. Bilinguals do not seem to compete with Swedish speakers in areas which demand knowledge of Swedish. Outside their own community, they also seem to have worse social possibilities than those who have Finnish as a dominant language. She finds a strong correlation between years of school and knowledge of Swedish, a fairly common finding in bilingual education research, although as she cautions, it may not be a causal relationship.

> The analysis leads us to the, according to our tests, most deprived, semilingual group among those interviewed. This group knows according to its own opinion Finnish better than Swedish, and Swedish poorly. They, however, did even worse in the Finnish test than the group which had studied Swedish as its major language . . .

> I would not like to argue that this group is aware of language problems in daily life. On the basis of short word tests it is difficult to draw any definite conclusions about the language competence of those interviewed. In addition, the languages within this group may be functionally differentiated. Probably this group is to be found mostly in occupations which are less demanding linguistically. (Jaakkola, 1974: 40)

Perrti Toukomaa's (1972) study on immigrant Finnish children supports the notion of semilingualism. Twelve-year-olds have the same vocabulary as eight-year-olds in Finland. 'Saddest is that their ability in Swedish is usually just as bad' (Toukomaa, 1972: 2). Those who were good in Swedish are usually those who had not forgotten their Finnish but developed the mother tongue. Of interest is his finding that the older the pupils when they immigrate, the better they can learn Swedish within a few years.

> According to results, one may expect that for a pupil who has come to Sweden as a four-year-old, it normally takes four to five years to achieve a passing understanding of the deeper meaning of words, while a pupil who has immigrated at the age of ten can manage the task in a couple of years. (Toukomaa, 1972: 4)

Although I am not sure of what he means with the deeper meaning of words, his results are certainly supported by those of Ervin-Tripp's (1974).

Predictably, the notion of semilingualism became polemic. Professor Loman (1974a) and his colleagues report on a number of studies in *Språk och Samhälle*, the major tenet of which is to do away with 'the myth of semilingualism'. The difficulty with the concept of semilingualism is that it is very vague in its linguistic definition and measurement, as Loman points out. He emphasizes the necessity of empirical studies, 'especially in the form of analyses of authentic language material'. He continues with an in-depth study of the informant from Tornedalen with the lowest social class index and, after a careful analysis of her ability to form correct sentences of a certain length, her fluency, and her lexicon, he concludes: 'If she is representative in her language ability — well, then the talk about semilingualism is based on fiction' (Loman, 1974b: 78).

Mirja Pinomaa (1974) examines 'Finnish interference in Tornedals Swedish' and Irina Koskinen (1974) 'Swedish interference in Tornedals Finnish' and both conclude by rejecting any evidence of semilingualism. Pinomaa also investigates the *meningsbyggnad*, 'the building of meaning', of 38 bilingual informants from Tornedalen, using the same criteria as Loman above, and concludes that her results do not support the notion of semilingualism. Kerstin Nordin (1974), following the same *Manual för Analys* (Loman & Jorgenson, 1971), compares the Swedish of 88 bilingual eighth graders with Finnish as the home language in Tornedalen with that of 26 bilingual native speakers of Swedish in Finland (Swedish and Finnish are both official languages in Finland). She concludes that one can find no linguistic handicap among the Swedish students.

We find again the familiar contradictory result of linguistic research on bilingual speakers, and I can only speculate on its meaning. All of the 'anti-semilingualism' studies have dealt with post-puberty informants (Swedish children begin school at seven years of age), and it seems likely that given sufficient exposure to Swedish, Finnish mother tongue speakers eventually learn to function well in that language. Everyone agrees that their Finnish is undeveloped in Haugen's (1972) sense of the term: they can neither read nor write Finnish, and they have difficulty understanding standard Finnish although there is no evidence that the language is not sufficient to meet the functional needs of the community in the diglossic situation which now exists. But no data exist on the language competence of young school children. The region is characterized by very rapid language shift with numerous reports on families shifting to Swedish after the first child or two. Anecdotal reports comment on the garbled Swedish — to the degree of incomprehensibility — of the parents, and it is reasonable to assume from the published data that a situation of interlanguage arose. I think it is a legitimate question to ask what kind of language competence children bring to school when they have never been exposed to a fully developed language. It is easy to fault the conceptualization of the last sentence, and I frankly admit that I cannot phrase it elegantly, but for the sake of the children we should at least consider the possible effect of semilingualism on early schooling.

Conclusions

I have attempted in this paper to examine the contradictory results of research studies on bilingual education from the viewpoint that we can only make sense of such research if we consider bilingual education as the *result of* societal factors rather than the *cause* of certain behavior in children. To that end, I have used Schermerhorn's theoretical framework for research on ethnic groups in contact and all too briefly touched upon Wallace's schema of revitalization movements. The conceptual framework of this paper shall necessarily need to become modified in light of further case studies, and I have not meant to imply that the notions I have introduced here will account for all aspects of bilingual education — rather I have meant to indicate the direction we should take in interpreting research on bilingual education.

Postscript

The notion of double semilingualism continued to interest me. When the National Swedish Board of Education asked me in 1982 to review the Swedish research and debate about bilingualism and bilingual education in Sweden, these were my conclusions about semilingualism (C.B. Paulston, 1982: 41–3):

Semilingualism

The notion of semilingualism was popularized in Sweden with the publication of Hansegård's *Tvåspråkighet eller halvspråkighet?* in 1968, but Ekstrand's (1981: 45 ff.) account of its previous history sounds credible. The term had its roots in the Finnish language struggle, surfaced in print in the press and always was a layman's term and never a theoretical concept. The term as any Swede will know refers to the imperfect learning of two languages, or to cite the Immigrant Bureau in Stockholm (Invandrarexpeditionen) *Invandrarundervisningen i Stockholms skolor,* 1979: 11 (The Education of Immigrants in Stockholm Schools): 'a poor Swedish which unfortunately lay the foundation for what we call semilingualism.'

The fact of the matter is that there is *no* empirical evidence to support the existence of such a language development hiatus as Hansegård claims. Linguist after linguist in Sweden (Hyltenstam & Stroud, 1982; Loman, 1974b; Oksaar, 1980; Stolt, 1975; Wande, 1977; Öhman, 1981) have criticized the notion. Loman specifically looked for evidence and found none. Nor did Ekvall (1979) or Nystål & Sjöberg (1976) or Rönmark & Wikström (1980).

The widespread mythology of semilingualism when there are no data is astounding to the outsider. Such mythology has obviously served a purpose: people believe what they want to. It has served as rationale for the Finnish groups in their demands for monolingual Finnish schooling in Sweden. It has also served as a rationale for the Swedish parents in Södertälje who do not want the Assyrian children in the same classes as their own children (Field notes, March 1972). There is anecdotal evidence that most immigrant parents wanted their children in mixed Swedish classes until they were informed about the dangers of semilingualism. In Hilmerson *et al.*'s (1980: 14) study, 61% of the Greek parents 'consider that there is a risk for semilingualism if the children do not receive home language instruction'. It is preferable to segregate children on the basis of preventing harm, i.e. semilingualism, than on the basis of racial discrimination, at least in Sweden. But I don't know what gave rise to the initial spread and general acceptance of the notion of semilingualism, and it certainly deserves a study. I expect the press may deserve part of the blame.

I also find it disconcerting that semilingualism is accepted as a bona fide theoretical concept in so many university student papers. The following quotations (which out of charity I won't identify) are typical and partially or totally inaccurate:

> These children lack any ability to express themselves fully in one language. . . . the consequences which may follow for the children to early add another language without properly having learned Finnish.

> Most researchers agree (*sic*) that submersion, i.e. when Finnish immigrant children are taught only in Swedish in Swedish class, can cause semilingualism.

They show a bias in critical thinking which has no place in academia. At the very least, one would expect a recognition and discussion of the controversial nature of such a notion.

I would like to conclude this part of the discussion by recommending that the notion of semilingualism not be used as a rationale for any of NBE's (National Board of Eduation) educational policies. It does not seem to exist.[1]

But I still wonder about White-Thunder.

Notes

General. With fifteen years' hindsight, it is easy to see that Schermerhorn's framework does not allow for regional nationalism, clearly the case with Quebec today. Social class is indeed not an issue, but independence, the francophone preferred term for separatism, is. Integration is not a popular concept in Quebec today and what the future will hold, no theoretical framework of ethnic relations will predict.

1. This is not to say that a child may not produce low scores on bilingual measures or tests, just as he would have produced low scores on monolingual measures. Any causal relationship between the two bilingual scores has not been demonstrated.

References

BLOOMFIELD, L. 1964, Literate and illiterate speech. In D. HYMES (ed.) *Language in Culture and Society*. New York: Harper and Row.

BRUDNER, L. 1973, The maintenance of bilingualism in southern Austria. *Ethnology* 11, 1.

CAMPBELL, R. 1970, English curricula for non-English speakers. In JAMES E. ALATIS (ed.) *Georgetown University Round Table on Languages and Linguistics 1970*. Washington, DC: Georgetown University Press.

—— 1972a, Bilingual education in Culver City. *Workpapers: Teaching English as a Second Language, 6* (pp. 87–92). Los Angeles: University of California.

—— 1972b, Bilingual education for Mexican–American children in California. In P. T. TURNER (ed.) *Bilingualism in the Southwest*. Tucson, Arizona: University of Arizona Press.

COHEN, A. 1974, The Culver City Spanish immersion program: the first two years. *The Modern Language Journal* 58, 95–103.

COHEN, A. D. and LEBACH, S. M. 1973, A language experiment in California: student, parent, and community reactions after three years. *Workpapers in Teaching English as a Second Language, 8*. Los Angeles: University of California.

EKSTRAND, L-H. 1981, Språk, identitet, kultur. *Reprints and Miniprints, 391*. Malmö: School of Education.

EKVALL, U. 1979, Ordval i skriftlig framställning hos 'invandrarelever' och svenska elever. Stockholm: University of Stockholm.

ENGLE, P. L. 1973, The use of the vernacular languages in education: revisited. (A literature review prepared for the Ford Foundation.) Later published (1975) as *The Use of Vernacular Languages in Education: Language Medium in Early School Years for Minority Language Groups.* Arlington, VA: Center for Applied Linguistics.

ERICKSON, D. 1969, *Community School at Rough Rock — An Evaluation for the Office of Economic Opportunity, US Department of Commerce.* Springfield, VA: Clearinghouse for Federal Scientific and Technical Information.

ERVIN-TRIPP, S. 1974, Is second language learning like the first? *TESOL Quarterly* 8, 2.

GAARDER, B. n.d., Political perspective on bilingual education. Manuscript. Washington, DC: US Office of Education.

HANSEGÅRD, N. E. 1968, *Tvåspråkighet eller halvspråkighet.* Stockholm: Aldus/ Bonniers.

HAUGEN, E. 1972, *Dialect, Language, Nation. The Ecology of Language.* Stanford: Stanford University Press.

HEATH, S. B. 1972, *Telling Tongues: Language Policy in Mexico: Colony to Nation.* New York: Teachers College Press.

HENRYSSON, S. and LJUNG, B-D. 1967, Tvåspråkigheten i Tornedalen. Unpublished report from Pedagogisk-psykologiska Institutionen. Lärarhögskolan i Stockholm, No. 26.

HILMERSON, B. *et al.* 1980, Attityder till språk och språkinlärning. Stockholm: University of Stockholm.

HYLTENSTAM, K. and STROUD, C. 1982, Halvspråkighet ett förbrukat slagord. *Invandrare och minoriteter* 3, 10–13.

HYMES, D. 1971, *Pidginization and Creolization of Languages.* Cambridge, MA: University Press.

The Institute of Education n.d., A mid-way report of the sixth-year primary project. Ife, West Nigeria: University of Ife.

Invandrarexpeditionen 1972, *Invandrarundervisningen i Stockholms skolor.* Stockholm.

JAAKKOLA, M. 1973, *Språkgränsen.* Stockholm: Bokförlag, Aldus.

—— 1974, Den språkliga variationen i svenska Tornedalen. In B. LOMAN (ed.) *Språk och Samhälle.* Lund: Gleerup.

KOSKINEN, I. 1974, Svensk interferens i Tornedalsfinskan. In B. LOMAN (ed.) *Språk och Samhälle.* Lund: Gleerup.

LAMBERT, W. E. and TUCKER, G. R. 1972, *Bilingual Education of Children: The St Lambert Experiment.* Rowley, MA: Newbury House.

LIEBERSON, S. 1970, *Language and Ethnic Relations in Canada.* New York: John Wiley and Sons.

LOMAN, B. (ed.) 1974a, *Språk och Samhälle.* Lund: Gleerup, Bokförlag.

—— 1974b, Till frågan om tvåspråkighet och halvspråkighet. *Språk och Samhälle.* Lund: Gleerup.

LOMAN, B. and JORGENSON, N. 1971, *Manual för analys och beskrivning av makrosyntagmer.* Lund: Lundastudier i nordisk språkvetenskap, Serie C, No, 1.

MACKEY, W. F. 1972, *Bilingual Education in a Binational School.* Rowley, MA: Newbury House.

MODIANO, N. 1966, Reading comprehension in the national language: A comparative study of bilingual and all Spanish approaches to reading instruction in

selected Indian schools in the highlands of Chiapas, Mexico. New York University: Unpublished doctoral dissertation.
—— 1973, *Indian Education in the Chiapas Highlands*. New York: Holt, Rinehart and Winston, 1973.
NORDIN, K. 1974, Meningsbyggnaden hos åttondeklassister i Övertorneå. *Språk och Samhälle*. Lund: Gleerup.
NYSTÅL, S. E. and SJÖBERG, T. 1976, Språktillhörighetskolprestation. Umeå: University of Umeå.
ÖHMAN, S. 1981, Halvspräkighet som Kastmärke. In *Att Leva med Mångfalden*. Stockholm: Liber.
OKSAAR, E. 1980, Tvåspråkighet i teori och praktik. *Invandrare och Minoriteter* 5–6, 43–7.
PAULSTON, C. B. 1975, *Implications of Language Learning Theory for Language Planning*. Arlington, VA: Center for Applied Linguistics.
—— 1982, *Swedish Research and Debate About Bilingualism*. Stockholm: Skolöverstyrelsen.
PAULSTON, R. G. 1971, Sociocultural constraints on educational development in Peru. *The Journal of Developing Areas* 5, 3.
—— 1972, Cultural revitalization and educational change in Cuba. *Comparative Education Review* 16, 3.
—— 1974, Ethnic revival and educational conflict in Swedish Lappland. Paper presented at the Conference of the American Anthropological Association, Mexico City, in *Comparative Education Review* 20, 2, 1976.
PELTO, P. 1970, *Anthropological Research: The Structure of Inquiry*. New York: Harper and Row.
PINOMAA, M. 1974, Finsk Interferens i Tornedalsfinskan. In B. LOMAN (ed.) *Språk och Samhälle 2*. Lund: Gleerup, Bokförlag.
PRATOR, C. 1966, Language policy in the primary school of Kenya. In B. W. ROBINETT (ed.) *On Teaching English to Speakers of Other Languages, Series III*. Washington, DC: TESOL.
RAMIREZ, A. n.d., Bilingual reading for speakers of Spanish: action research and experimentation. (Mimeo.)
RAMOS, M., AGUILAR, T. and SIBAYAN, B. 1967, *The Determination and Implementation of Language Policy*. Quezon City: Phoenix Press.
RINGBOM, H. 1962, Tvåspråkigheten som forskningsobjekt. *Finsk Tidskrift*, 6.
RÖNMARK, W. and WIKSTRÖM, J. 1980, *Tvåspråkighet i Tornedalen*. Umeå: University of Umeå.
SCHERMERHORN, R. A. 1970, *Comparative Ethnic Relations: A Framework for Theory and Research*. New York: Random House.
STOLT, B. 1975, Om 'halvspråkighet' och 'språkighets känslofunktion'. *Noridsh Minoritetsforskining* 2, 1, 5–12.
SWAIN, M. 1974, Some issues in bilingual education in Canada. Paper presented at Indiana University. Manuscript.
SWAIN, M. and BARIK, H. C. 1978, Bilingual education in Canada: French and English. In B. SPOLSKY and R. L. COOPER (eds) *Case Studies in Bilingual Education*. Rowley, Mass.: Newbury House, 22–71.
TENERZ, H. 1966, *Språkundervisnings problemen i de finsktalande delarna av Norrbottenslän*. Lund: Gleerup.

34   BILINGUAL EDUCATION: SOCIOLINGUISTIC PERSPECTIVES

TOUKOMAA, P. 1972, Om finska invandrarelevernas utvecklingsförhållanden i den svenska skolan. Beteende-vetenskapliga Institutionen, Uleåborgs Universitet.
VERDOODT, A. 1972, The differential impact of immigrant French speakers on indigenous German speakers: a case study in the light of two theories. In J. A. FISHMAN (ed.) *Advances in the Sociology of Language, Part II*. The Hague: Mouton.
WALLACE, A. 1966, Revitalization movements. *American Anthropologist 59*.
WANDE, E. 1977, Hansegård är ensidig. *Invandrare och Minoriteter*, 3–4, 44–51.

3 Language and Ethnic Boundaries[1]

Recently, in examining a colleague's research on the Canadian immersion programs, it struck me forcibly what a bother the Canadian language situation is, what a tremendous outpouring of energy and money — and strife. I commented how much easier it would all be if the Franco-Canadians would just give up their French. My colleague looked at me quizzically, grinned, and said, 'Of course.' Now, that simple exchange illustrates a number of issues that need to be considered in a discussion of bilingualism.

The reason for her initial puzzlement was that she for a moment took my remark as a scholarly statement about optative language policy goals for French-speaking Canada, although she knew very well that I was a supporter of cultural pluralism and concomitant bilingual education. In other words, she was well acquainted with the particular bias with which I approach bilingualism and bilingual education. I am in favor of it. It is not only *my* bias; it is shared by every linguist and anthropologist I know of who does scholarly work on bilingualism and bilingual education. In all likelihood, it is a bias which is shared by most if not all of the participants at this first Scandinavian Conference on Bilingualism. It is not a bias for which I apologize; rather I find it totally justified. But there is the crux; the burden is upon me to demonstrate such a justification and to do so on the basis of data and empirical facts. I find much writing and research on bilingualism and bilingual education flawed by a lack of objectivity, which influences the research designs as well as leads to unwarranted conclusions and speculations. This conference is an appropriate time to acknowledge our bias, because it is only by acknowledging it that we can adequately control for it in our work as well as allow the reader a more accurate interpretation of our scholarly opinions.

Once my colleague realized what I meant, she agreed. Language diversity within nations frequently leads to a number of problems, especially in the educational sector, which may not occur in a monolingual state. Attempts at solutions frequently carry a high economic cost, e.g. federal funding alone in the United States for bilingual education in 1977 is $118 million. A common rejoinder among my colleagues is 'Good, let them build one less atomic submarine'. In other words, the perception and evaluation of the social results of ethnic groups in contact become a matter of priorities. It is undeniable, just as my colleague did not attempt to deny it, that social life in Canada would be simpler with only one language. But to her mind as to mine, increased efficacy and economy of communication do not justify the enforced loss of cultural identity and way of life of a people, a choice of priorities which ultimately is based on moral values.

Frequently reason has little to do with attempts at solutions. It is not reasonable for students to riot and get killed because the authorities want to teach one language rather than another in the schools, yet I think we all understand the Black reaction to the introduction of Afrikaans instead of English in South Africa. Afrikaans is a very powerful symbol for the hated oppression, and as I write this, the riots are continuing. Clearly Afrikaans in and by itself was not the real reason behind the revolt, but rather the reason lay in the nature of the relationship between the subordinate Blacks and the dominant whites. In our discussions of bilingualism and bilingual situations, we need to recognize that often the problem has nothing or little to do with language *per se*.

The present language situation in the province of Quebec is a result of a power struggle between the economically dominant Anglo Canadians and the politically dominant Franco Canadians. Through legal measures, the French have been able to enforce a knowledge of French as a requisite for access to a number of jobs. As a result, about 50% of the English-speaking children in Montreal enter kindergarten in French immersion programs (programs in which French is used as a medium of instruction), with the hope by their parents that they will learn sufficient French in school to be able to qualify for future positions. Language is used by the French as a mechanism for maintaining ethnic boundaries in order to deny English-speaking Canadians access to scarce jobs.

Language can similarly be used for the maintenance of ethnic boundaries in order to keep members within the group. The trilingual Old Order Amish is an example of a group who uses language for the maintenance of group boundaries both to keep their members in and outsiders out. The Pennsylvania Old Order Amish is a Protestant religious group characterized by:

> horse and buggies for transportation, no electricity in their homes, farm animals for farming, the occupation most engaged in, education only to the eighth grade, plain dress, refusal to accept government benefits such as social security, and the use of Pennsylvania Dutch, a

> German dialect from the speech of German Rhenish Palatinate, German, and English. (Yoder, 1976: 2–3)

German is used for sermons, prayers, and bible reading from the Luther Bible, the 1534 translation from the Latin. Since Pennsylvania law requires school attendance until 15, many Old Order Amish spend an additional year after eighth grade in a special intensive program learning German, thus fulfilling the legal requirement while serving their own purpose. English is learnt in school and is used in any exchange with 'English' or 'gay' persons, as non-members are referred to. English is also used for non-religious reading. Pennsylvania Dutch is the mother tongue and is spoken in the home, always at church-related social activities, and often to other church members even in the 'English' world, such as in the grocery store (Yoder, 1976). Members have a strong feeling that

> German is the better form of the language, richer, deeper, more capable of expressing deep thoughts than either Pennsylvania Dutch or English. The deep thoughts in one's life are those relating to God. So take away German, and one has taken away that aspect of his life. (Yoder, 1976: 10)

For the deeply religious Amish, it is clear that the functional distribution of language use contributes to the motivation for staying within the church and for resisting the obvious temptations to join one of the less conservative churches, like that of the Mennonites, who do not have the same extreme restrictions on daily life. Nor do the Mennonites make similar use of language and indeed their present day high school generation is monolingual in English.

In this paper, I would like to examine the phenomenon of group bilingualism, the origin of the contact situations which led to it, and the role of language in maintaining ethnic boundaries, especially in revitalization movements. We need to examine such issues because we will never be able to understand the nature of bilingualism if we consider it as a uniform phenomenon. Bilingualism may be a universal condition but it serves a variety of functions which need to be considered for an adequate understanding of the social consequences of group bilingualism. Furthermore, group bilingualism more often than not is not stable, and becomes the major mechanism of language shift, a phenomenon which is poorly understood (Fishman, 1966; Lieberson, Dalto & Johnston, 1975). Revitalization movements are likely to be a mechanism for language maintenance or language revival. Language shift and language maintenance, with or without concomitant bilingualism, are of course indicators of the degree to which ethnic boundaries are being maintained.

Gaarder (n.d.) makes the crucial distinction between elitist bilingualism and folk bilingualism. Elitist bilingualism is the hallmark of intellectuals and the learned in most societies and, one might add, of upper-class membership in many societies as it certainly is in Scandinavia. It is a matter of choice. Not so with folk bilingualism which is the result of ethnic groups in contact and competition within a single state, where 'one of the peoples become bilingual involuntarily in order to survive' (Gaarder, n.d.: 4). Elitist bilingualism is not likely to be a mechanism for language shift or maintenance, and in this paper I will consider only folk bilingualism.

In an earlier paper (C. B. Paulston, 1975b), I drew on Schermerhorn's (1970) 'Inductive typology' of *Comparative Ethnic Relations* in an attempt to analyze the consequences of bilingual education in North America, the direct result of ethnic groups in contact, and I would like briefly to review it here. Schermerhorn (1970: 68) points out that 'the probability is overwhelming that when two groups with different cultural histories establish contacts that are regular rather than occasional or intermittent, one of the two groups will typically assume dominance over the other', and he says elsewhere (Schermerhorn, 1972: 379 ff.) it is the nature of this dominance which is the major factor in ethnic relations. The central question then in comparative research in ethnic relations (immediate causal factor of a group's bilingual status) is 'what are the conditions that foster or prevent the integration of ethnic groups into their environing societies?' (Schermerhorn, 1970: 14). The percentage of members of a group who become bilingual can be seen as a concomitant condition of the degree of integration. Schermerhorn sees three major causal factors as determining the nature of the relationship between ethnic groups and the process of integration into the environing society. The first refers to the origin of the contact situation between 'the subordinate ethnic and dominant groups, such as annexation, migration, and colonization,' the second to 'the degree of enclosure (institutional separation or segmentation) of the subordinate group or groups from the society-wide network of institutions and associations', and the third to 'the degree of control exercised by dominant groups over access to scarce resources by subordinate groups in a given society' (Schermerhorn, 1970: 15).

Liberson, Dalto & Johnston (1975) in a quantificationally very sophisticated article on 'The course of mother-tongue diversity in nations' point out the failure of developmental factors, such as urbanization, to account for cross-national changes in language diversity. They consider the very rapid language shift in the United States:

> For the descendants of literally tens of millions of immigrants, English
> became the mother tongue in a matter of a few generations (Lieberson

and Curry, 1971). It is reasonable to ask how it came about that the shift was so rapid in the United States compared with that in the vast majority of nations. (Lieberson, Dalto & Johnston, 1975: 53)

They conclude, like Schermerhorn, that one must consider the origin of the contact situation and go on to 'develop a theory which suggests that the course of race and ethnic relations will be different in settings where the subordinate group is indigenous as opposed to those where the migrant populations are subordinate'. They consider, similarly to Schermerhorn to whom they refer, four groups: (1) indigenous superordinate, (2) migrant superordinate, (3) indigenous subordinate, and (4) migrant subordinate. They find it unlikely that much, if any, mother tongue shift will occur among the first two groups.

> Almost certainly a group enjoying both political and economic dominance will be in a position to ensure that its linguistic position is maintained. Bilingualism may occur, but this is not the same as mother-tongue shift: At the very most, one can normally expect only an extremely slow rate of mother-tongue change among such groups. (Lieberson, Dalto & Johnston, 1975: 53)

The role of Swedish in Finland illustrates that point and gives us an example of an ethnic group in demographic and political decline which uses its native tongue to maintain its boundaries for ethnic survival (R. G. Paulston, 1976b). Like the English-speaking Canadians in Quebec, the Swedish-speaking Finns lack political power in Finland and so are vulnerable to any legal measures the Finnish-speaking majority might institute in regard to Swedish. Presumably the status of Swedish as a lingua franca in Scandinavia (Skutnabb-Kangas, 1975) and strong feelings of Scandinavian solidarity have contributed to the Finns' tolerance toward Swedish, but its continued role in Finland is best explained by the former superordinate status of its mother tongue speakers.

Subordinate groups who are indigenous at the time of contact, either through colonization as in the case of the American Indians or through annexation as in the case of the Chicanos in the US southwest, are unlikely to change rapidly. Migrant subordinate groups are the only groups likely to show rapid rates of mother tongue shift, as the recent migrant Finnish working-class population in Sweden illustrates in so rapid a shift that there is anecdotal evidence of difficulties of communication between parents and children. In the United States, as Lieberson, Dalto & Johnston (1975) show, the immigrant experience was one of extra-ordinarily rapid shift. In contrast, within the same nation and with access to the same educational institution of public schooling, the indigenous subordinate groups have changed at a much slower rate. In 1940, 20% of the whites in Louisiana still reported French as their mother tongue although the state had been purchased from France almost 150 years before, in 1803. In New Mexico, conquered in 1846, nearly 45% of the native parentage population (third or later generation) reported also in 1940, Spanish as their mother tongue, which means that, since a fair proportion of this population was not of Spanish origin, much more than half of the Spanish-speaking population had not shifted (Lieberson, Dalto & Johnston, 1975). In contrast to Louisiana, the southwest has a steady trickle of new immigrants, legal and illegal, from Mexico, and no one really knows the exact rate of language shift, but Thompson (1974) calculates that in Texas Spanish has remained the mother tongue for 80% of the third generation.

The Indian population probably has been the slowest to become bilingual. Lieberson, Dalto & Johnston (1975) cite census data which show that as recently as 1900 slightly more than 40% of the Indian population could not speak English. Many of those who did speak English also maintained their Indian mother tongue. They (1975: 56) conclude that 'it is clear that mother-tongue shift was far slower than for the subordinate immigrant groups'.

The degree to which these populations become bilingual in mother tongue and English varies, and the fact that many don't has resulted in national recognition of that problem in the form of federal legislation of the so-called Bilingual Education Act of 1968. The official intent of this act is the more efficient teaching of English through the transitional use of the mother tongue. The implementation of these programs, as I have written about elsewhere (C. B. Paulston, 1977), is accompanied by considerable strife by school personnel who cite their own immigrant experience background as example that there is no need for bilingual education. The militant minority ethnic groups, the Chicanos, the Puerto Ricans, the Navajos, refuse to accept the assimilationist goals of the programs, and instead talk about (and where they can, implement) bilingual/bicultural maintenance programs. It is a clear group conflict situation, played out in the educational sector, where the ethnic groups are insisting on their rights to maintain their ethnic boundaries, much to the disapproval of the dominant Anglos.

These findings on language shift through a bilingual generation and language maintenance with or without concomitant bilingualism raise some issues which are important for a more accurate understanding of the nature of bilingualism. They also illustrate, I think, the importance of a comparative approach in this field of study. The first question which comes to mind is why would the immigrant experience result in such rapid language shift with no apparent educational problems when the indigenous groups encountered such difficulties; why have the latter maintained their mother tongue and what is the mechanism of language maintenance? It is clear, I think, that the mechanism of language shift in the United States has been bilingualism:

> Immigrant languages disappear because they do not transfer from one generation to the next. Typically in the United States the first generation prefers to speak the non-English tongue, the second generation is bilingual, and the third claims English as its mother tongue, learning the immigrant language mainly through contact with the grandparents. The Spanish language seems to be an exception. (Thompson, 1974: 7)

What is not clear are the factors which resulted in the language maintenance or slow rate of shift of the indigenous populations. Just what is the role of mother tongue language in the ethnic minority groups and why do these groups insist on maintenance bilingual programs rather than accept the transitional assimilation goals? In the remainder of the paper, I shall attempt to deal with these issues.

Language shift can be seen as an indicator of integration into the environing society, and we can rephrase the first question slightly: why did the immigrants to the United States integrate into the larger society more rapidly and completely than did the indigenous groups? As Lieberson, Dalto & Johnston point out, one reason was that the indigenous groups already had a set of social and cultural institutions *in situ* through which they attempted to pursue their preconquest activities. Another reason was that they tended to be spatially isolated.

These two reasons are both subsumed under Schermerhorn's variable of degree of enclosure. The less the two groups share socio-cultural institutions like the same churches, the same schools, the same jobs, the higher the degree of enclosure within that society. Schermerhorn (1970: 124) points out that we do not have a very clear idea of the degree of enclosure of plural societies which are the result of annexation. In plural societies, 'institutions of kinship, religion, the economy, education, recreation and the like are parallel but different in structure and norms. Ordinarily this is compounded by differences in language and sometimes by race as well.' The relationship between degree of enclosure and the role of language in ethnic boundary maintenance processes is not understood, and I cannot think of any study which has examined this particular problem. Clearly it is an important topic for future investigation.

The degree of control by the Anglo dominant group over access to goods and services also influenced the situation. The contact situations within the same nation between the Anglo Americans and the Chicanos, the Puerto Ricans, the Amerindians, were all the result of military conquest. The Chicanos were segregated to one part of town and given access only to menial type jobs. The Indians were isolated on reservations where no opportunity for jobs existed. The immigrants, on the other hand, were given access to jobs. Brudner's (1972) thesis that jobs select language learning strategies is one that I have never found an exception to. When jobs were available which required a knowledge of English, the ethnic minority members became bilingual. Without access to rewards, English was and is not salient.

Schermerhorn also posits three intervening or contextual variables which modify the effect of the independent variables. The most important is the agreement or disagreement between dominant and subordinate groups on collective goals for the latter, such as assimilation or pluralism. Schermerhorn (1970: 85) sets up a paradigm of which one purpose is to 'specify the social contexts that can serve as intervening variables in answer to the scientific query, "under what conditions?"'. He bases his discussion on Wirth's typology of the different policies adopted by minority groups in response to their unprivileged position.

> These policies he called assimilationist, pluralist, secessionist, and militant. Briefly, assimilationist policy seeks to merge the minority members into the wider society by abandoning their own cultural distinctiveness and adopting their superordinates' values and style of life. The pluralist strategy solicits tolerance from the dominant group that will allow the subordinates to retain much of their cultural distinctiveness. The secessionist minority aims to separate or detach itself from the superordinates so as to pursue an independent existence. Finally, the militants . . . intend to gain control over the dominants who currently have the ascendency. (Schermerhorn, 1970: 78)

Schermerhorn points out that assimilation and pluralism really refer to cultural aspects while secession and militancy refer to structural.

> To clarify this problem it is well to insist on the analytic distinction between culture and social structure. Culture signifies the ways of action learned through socialization, based on norms and values that serve as guides or standards for that behavior. Social structure, on the other hand, refers to 'the set of crystallized social relationships which its (the society's) members have with each other which places them in groups, large or small, permanent or temporary, formally organized or unorganized, and which relates them to the major institutional activities of the society, such as economic and occupational life, reli-

gion, marriage and the family, education, government, and recreation' (Gordon, 1964: 30–1). (Schermerhorn, 1970: 80)

In order to deal with the difficulty of applying cultural features to conditions which involve social features, he suggests the paired concepts of centripetal and centrifugal trends in social life. 'Centripetal tendencies refer both to cultural trends such as acceptance of common values, styles of life, etc., as well as structural features like increased participation in a common set of groups, associations, and institutions' (Schermerhorn 1970: 81). To keep the two aspects distinct, he calls the first assimilation, the latter incorporation.

> Centrifugal tendencies among subordinate groups are those that foster separation from the dominant group or from societal bonds in one respect or another. Culturally this most frequently means retention and preservation of the group's distinctive traditions in spheres like language, religion, recreation, etc., together with the particularistic values associated with them: Wirth's cultural requirements are needed, so there are demands for endogamy, separate associations, and even at times a restricted range of occupations. (Schermerhorn, 1970: 81–2)

Schermerhorn's major point is that integration, which involves the satisfaction of the ethnic group's modal tendency, whether it be centripetal or centrifugal, depends on the agreement or congruence of views by the dominant and subordinate groups on the goals of the latter as shown by Figure 3.1.

The immigrants' goals were clearly those of assimilation; they had voluntarily left 'the old country', with its frequently unsatisfactory conditions, behind. The indigenous groups, in contrast, did not seek contact with the dominant Anglos but found it imposed on them; their groups in their entirety were brought into the environing society with their culture intact. Today many subordinate ethnic groups in the United States do not want to abandon their cultural distinctiveness; rather they want access to goods and services, to the institutional privileges held by the English-speaking middle class, i.e. economic incorporation but not assimilation. One important aspect of resisting assimilation is the maintenance of the mother tongue, in the same way as language shift is an important aspect of assimilation.

The goals for all non-English-speaking groups as seen by the dominant group have always been assimilation, the acceptance of 'the American creed,' the socialization into American ways and values. Since this was also the goal of the immigrants, they willingly acquiesced to the assimilation process, and the relationship between the dominant group and the immigrants

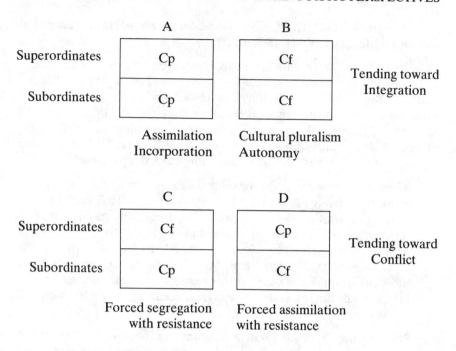

Cp = Centripetal trends
Cf = Centrifugal trends

Source: Schermerhorn, 1970: 83

FIGURE 3.1   *Congruent and incongruent orientations toward centripetal and centrifugal trends of subordinates as viewed by themselves and superordinates*

is best characterized by Cell A, a situation tending toward integration. Anything less became considered unpatriotic, and I have more than once when I criticized some feature of American life been told 'if you don't like it here, why don't you go back to where you came from'.

The indigenous groups, on the other hand, tended to resist assimilation, and their situation is symbolized by Cell D. It is slight wonder that, in a situation characterized by conflict, in which they resisted assimilation at the same time as they were denied access to goods and services and were separated institutionally from the English-speaking group, members of indigenous groups did not shift to English to the same degree and at the same rate as the immigrant group. The degree to which the indigenous groups became bilingual probably depended mostly on access to jobs which required a knowledge of English; the degree to which they maintained the mother tongue probably depended most on the resistance against assimilation. The affluent Amish, who are an exception to the immigrant experience of rapid language shift, exemplify both these points. They are perfectly bilingual as their business dealings with the 'gay' world necessitate a knowledge of English, which they learn primarily in the public schools. They have stubbornly resisted assimilation into American mainstream culture for religious reasons and not only have they maintained the mother tongue but also add standard German as an additional language, crucial to the transmittance of the group's basic values.

However, the use of census data to establish language shift as Lieberson, Dalto & Johnston do masks the variation of language use between the various immigrant groups. Furthermore, assimilation is not necessarily an irreversible process. The United States has lately experienced a resurgence of ethnic awareness which brings into question the goal of complete assimilation for these ethnic groups. Elazar & Friedman (1976) discuss this new development of ethnic reaffirmation in American society in their perceptive *Moving Up: Ethnic Succession in America*. They point out that ethnic identity has often been seen as a problem that must somehow be overcome. Social scientists have often considered religious and ethnic groups as 'vestiges of a primitive past that are destined to disappear' (Elazar & Friedman, 1976: 4), but recent 'writers on the "new pluralism" have argued that racial, religious, and ethnic groups *are* a basic component of our social structure' (Elazar & Friedman, 1976: 5) who affect our institutions and at times are more powerful than economic forces in their influence.

As a result of the migration process, there has been a pattern of ethnic division of labor in the United States; e.g. the Irish have been drawn to local politics and civil service, the Slavic groups constitute a large part of labor in the coal mines and steel mills, while the Jews have been active *inter alia* in family style businesses. Elazar & Friedman point out that large groups within the American populace continue to be 'ethnic outs' in 'various stages of their own struggle to become "ethnic ins"'. These groups of Italian, Slovak, Polish, Jewish, Greek, Hungarian and Ukranian background 'are still struggling for recognition, upward mobility and the preservation of modest gains laboriously achieved after years of struggle' (Elazar & Friedman, 1976: 19). It is no coincidence that (with the exception of Jewish which is not a language) all of those languages are still natively spoken in Pittsburgh and mark group boundaries which are isomorphic with limited access to social rewards.

The capacity of the 'outs' to change their status, say Elazar & Friedman (1976: 14) depend on their potential social and political power, their willingness to use unorthodox tactics, the extent of opposition, and their ability to evoke sympathy. They have before them the example of the Blacks. Black gains during the 1960s and 1970s came about through ethnic solidarity and 'were obtained primarily through the institutionalization of their own political strength' (Elazar & Friedman, 1976: 15), which during the 1960s resulted in highly visible ethnic confrontations. The results of these ethnic confrontations led other groups to make demands — as groups. These demands came at a difficult time.

> From post-World War II through the late 1960s, America sustained rapid expansion and development of what has been called 'the metropolitan frontier.' There was a dramatic use of social, economic, and technical opportunities which the civil rights movement helped blacks to be able to take advantage of. Jobs, status and the good things of life were within the reach of growing numbers of Americans in an expanding economy. (Elazar & Friedman 1976: 21)

This expansion has now come to an end, and the present recession has exacerbated poverty and joblessness among the minorities. Unemployment has contributed to ethnic solidarity as the experience seems to show that competition for rewards is more successful when carried out by groups than by individuals, and the group boundaries have been those of ethnicity (R. G. Paulston, 1976c).

One resource of ethnic groups which can be used in stressing ethnic awareness and identity of the members is the original mother tongue. Pittsburgh radio stations, as do others in the country, carry radio programs in Italian, Slovak, Croatian, etc. The Slovak community here, for example, offers a non-formal course in Slovak culture, cuisine, music and language. Its students are from all social classes and all ages. Many Polish (for instance) families are changing their surname from the anglofied version back to the original Polish. At the University of Pittsburgh, a number of students of Polish, Greek, Hungarian, etc. background, who have completely shifted to English, are laboriously studying the language of their grandparents. Clearly this language learning will serve no immediate practical purpose, but it does serve to reaffirm their ethnic identity and to reinforce old boundaries which in their case had become eliminated.

The most extreme form of ethnic mobilization occurs in what Wallace (1956: 265) has termed revitalization movements, 'deliberate, organized, conscious efforts by members of a society to construct a more satisfying culture'. For Wallace, this process involves a cultural transformation of the group. For the purposes of this paper, I will extend the term to include ethnic revival movements as well (which may not be involved in a cultural transformation) since Wallace's (1975: 22–3) concept of 'revolutionary phase' applies to both movements.

In his 'Schools in revolutionary and conservative societies', Wallace (1975) discusses the learning priorities of the two types of society:

> What a man is expected to do in his life will, in part, depend on whether he lives in a revolutionary, conservative, or reactionary society and what he is expected to do determines what he is expected to learn. (Wallace, 1975: 21)

He outlines the model of learning priorities shown in Figure 3.2.

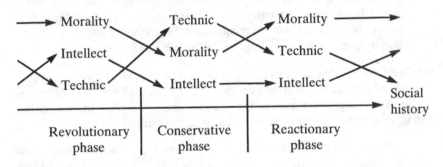

Source: Wallace (1975: 26)

FIGURE 3.2 *Learning priorities in revolutionary, conservative, and reactionary societies*

Wallace assigns very specific meanings to the terms *technic, morality* and *intellect*. By technic he refers to learning as a process of 'reliability increase of action' through stimulus, reinforcement and motivation; technic is learning 'how to'. Morality, on the other hand, stresses 'what'. Morality concerns one particular kind of socially approved value:

> This kind of value is the conception that one's own behaviour, as well as the behaviour of others, should not merely take into consideration the attitude of the community, but should actively advance, or at least not retard, its welfare. (Wallace, 1975: 18)

Although most commonly practiced in the humble endurance of discomfort by inconspicuous people, it is 'most conspicuously exemplified by such heroic actions as the soldier's throwing himself on a handgrenade in order to smother the blast and save his buddies' (Wallace, 1975: 18). The criterion for morality is its potential for sacrifice, and all ethnic groups in the revolutionary phase have sacrificial heroes as leaders, i.e. leaders who are willing to risk freedom or life for the cause; Cesar Chavez and La Causa is a good example.

By intellect, Wallace refers to Jacques Barzun's (1959) metaphor in *The House of Intellect* as an 'establishment'. Wallace cites Barzun:

> From the image of a house and its economy, one can see what an inquiry into the institution of Intellect must include. The main topics are: the state of the language, the system of schooling, the means and objects of communication, the supplies of money for thought and learning, and the code of feeling and conduct that goes with them. When the general tendency of these arrangements makes for order, logic, clarity, and speed of communication, one may say that a tradition of Intellect exists. (Wallace, 1975: 19)

Wallace (1975: 20) concludes his discussion of intellect by pointing out that it is the only truly universal tool which is 'capable of maintaining and restoring human arrangements against the erosions of time, capable of recognizing and solving new problems as well as learning answers to old ones'.

A group, like the Nation of Islam (in common parlance often referred to as the Black Muslims), or an entire society, like Cuba, may enter a revolutionary phase when they perceive their present circumstances and state of affairs as intolerable to support further. The regressive response of individuals in the stage preceding a revitalization movement typically includes 'alcoholism, extreme passivity and indolence, the development of highly ambivalent dependency relationships, intragroup violence, disregard of kinship and sexual mores, irresponsibility in public officials, states of depression and self-reproach, and probably a variety of psychosomatic and neurotic disorders' (Wallace, 1956: 269). It is no accident that abstinence, hard work, independence, black brotherhood, the importance of the family unit, responsibility, and Black pride are some of the values most revered by members of the Nation of Islam (Mohammad, 1976).

As is typical and necessary in revitalization movements, the Nation of Islam has its charismatic leaders, especially the late Elijah Mohammad, who formulated 'the nature of the existing culture's deficiencies, the nature of a desirable goal culture, and the nature and mode of operation of the transfer culture. This formulation must be more than an exercise of intellect: it must be passionately moral' (Wallace 1975: 22). It speaks for the explicatory

LANGUAGE AND ETHNIC BOUNDARIES 49

power of Wallace's theoretical framework of revitalization movements that
it was formulated years before the creation of the Nation of Islam, yet it perfectly accounts for its development.

Groups undergoing a revolutionary phase will always stress moral
learning, and conflicts are certain to arise when a revitalization movement
takes place within a conservative society where technic has the highest learning priority, i.e. 'in conservative societies, schools prepare people not for
sacrifice but for jobs' (R. G. Paulston, 1972: 478). Indeed, wherever possible, the Nation of Islam has its own private schools in order to be able to
implement its own learning priorities of 'moral transformation of the population' (Wallace, 1975: 23). The success of a revitalization movement within
a larger society, such as the economic and cultural success of the Nation of
Islam, depends on the larger society's tolerance for cultural pluralism. The
extreme respectability of the members in dress and an emphasis on moral
values which are not in conflict with those of the mainstream culture presumably have contributed to this success. Nor has there been any attempt to use
language, so called non-standard Negro English or Black English, in the
process of defining the group's new identity.

The success of the Nation of Islam contrasts sharply with the fate of
another Black revitalization movement, the Black Panther Party. The second learning priority in a revolutionary phase is intellect and, says Wallace,
the moral intellectuals often appear as fanatics to the conservative society.
It is interesting to speculate that the failure of the Black Panthers partially
was due to an emphasis on intellect rather than on morality and to the lack
of a consistently outlined goal culture as the Nation of Islam very carefully
had done:

> The Panthers, however, like many other groups before them had a
> number of shortcomings. Probably the main one was the lack of a
> thorough radical analysis and coupling that with a strong, organized set
> of strategies and programs. As with many other groups, publicity and
> their image may have clouded their own ideas of what they wanted to
> do. But, when as they sometimes seemed to be doing, the leadership
> changed its views so often, with not enough outside feedback to guide
> them, they did amazingly well . . . (Mason, 1976: 56)

The very point is that leadership in revitalization movements is messianic
and does not depend on outside feedback, nor is the moral teaching of goals
frequently changed. The Black Panthers were militant; they carried loaded
weapons while still legal; cited Malcolm X, the assassinated Black leader,
Mao Tse-tung and Marx; and some with Eldridge Cleaver called for under-
ground terrorist-type activities. Huey Newton, a cofounder, titled his book

(1972) *To Die for the People: The Writings of Huey P. Newton*. The larger society considered them as fanatics and showed no tolerance: Cleaver went eventually into exile for many years, and Newton was jailed for the murder of a policeman (he was freed in 1970 after two years in jail). Says Mason (1976: 24), 'The trial of Huey P. Newton itself is regarded by many educators, as well as lawyers, ordinary black citizens, etc. as truly revealing the racist character of the legal system'.

The writings of the Black Panthers are also in impeccable standard English, but in their speeches there are occasional occurrences of Black English for stylistic effect, to mark group solidarity. Ethnic groups typically use its mother tongue or dialect to such purpose, and the reluctance in both Black revitalization movements to use Black English reflects its stigmatized status as a former creole. To members of the Nation of Islam, Black English is associated with the conditions of life before their cultural transformation and plays no part in the group's moral teaching. It should be recognized that this is an unusual situation in revitalization movements.

Language skills in the official language can ordinarily be seen as an aspect of technic, an aspect of preparation for jobs, which is the major priority of learning in a conservative society. The mother tongue, on the other hand, is an aspect of moral learning, reaffirming the solidarity and cultural uniqueness of the ethnic group, underscoring the need to teach the moral values of good and evil, right and wrong, the values of the old gods, in the language in which those values were originally transmitted. Reaffirmation of cultural values are frequently a part of the moral teaching, especially among ethnic groups who prior to the revitalization movement have been taught by the dominant group to have nothing but contempt for their own culture.

The conflict over learning priorities explains the extreme importance of control over local educational institutions. I have frequently heard commented among my colleagues that the best bilingual schools are those that are under community control — be it Navajo or Chicano. I am not certain what 'best' means in this connection. In my discussion of the Erickson *et al.* (1969) report in an earlier paper (C. B. Paulston, 1975a: 25), I pointed out that 'rhetoric about cultural pluralism accounts for little if the objectives are not implemented'; the community-run Navajo school, as measured by the achievement test batteries from the California Test Bureau, was markedly inferior to the government-run school academically. I was at the time only interested in investigating the learning of English language skills, but even so that statement — and the evaluation itself — shows our typical tendency to assess and evaluate the schooling of groups undergoing a revitalization movement with moral learning as the priority, in terms of the standards of the conservative society — the standards of technic.

The following case study of 'Ethnic revival and educational conflict in Swedish Lapland' (R. G. Paulston, 1976a) illustrates the importance of autonomy over educational programs by the group in a revitalization phase. It illustrates once again the tendency to intolerance of cultural pluralism by the larger society except when it sees its own purposes furthered; consistently, when the national economy favored reindeer herding, the collective goals for the Saami as seen by Swedish officials included the use of Saami and support of Saami culture; otherwise, the goals were Swedish and assimilation. We also see here the typical support (maintenance and/or revival) of the mother tongue in ethnic revival movements.

Swedish government relations with the Saami began with the Lappmark edict of 1673 which sought to open the Saami's traditional homeland to Swedish settlers and the State Church.[2] This document promulgated a policy of minority integration, along with descriptions of stereotypical minority attributes, that has continued in large part down to the present day (cited in Ruong, 1969b: 203). It states that:

(1) Lapps should devote themselves to reindeer breeding in the mountain areas, a task for which they are best suited.

(2) Swedish settlers should have the right to take land from the Forest Lapps, to hunt and fish on Lapp lands, and to burn and clear Lapp land.

(3) The Lapps are a barbaric people from elsewhere without legal title to the land they use. They are lazy and useless in war.

In the following centuries, two themes pervaded ethnic relations. The dominant theme called for Saami to withdraw before the advance of Western economic penetration. Saami might indeed join this advance by rejecting their language and other core cultural traditions and becoming Swedes.

The second and lesser theme, that the Saami minority should be preserved and protected, largely through paternalistic efforts of the Swedish State Church, became increasingly important in the nineteenth century as traditional Saami nomad society disintegrated under the onslaught of expanding Scandinavian societies. With a cultural-revitalization movement led by the minister Lars Laestadius, the ensuring strengthening of social responsibility, and the increased value of reindeer herding in the national economy, educational policy for the Saami shifted emphasis from acculturation to socialized isolation (Nordberg, 1956; Ruong, 1969b). By about World War I, what might be called the 'conservationist' ideology had gained predominance and became embodied in the Normal School Reform of 1913. The Act's rationale, both economic and educational, is clearly apparent in the position stated by the Bishop of Luleå, a leader of the school reform and the religious head of the Saami (cited in Ruong, 1969b: 142):

> Lapps lack the physical attributes necessary for regular, heavy manual labor and therefore fall into deep poverty and misery when they adopt a settled way of life. If, on the other hand, they continue with reindeer breeding, they can count upon a secure source of livelihood. It is, accordingly, of national economic interest that the Lapps retain their inherited source of livelihood.

The vast tundra and mountain areas of Northern Scandinavia could, at that time, be most economically exploited as pasture for reindeer, and herding required that the Saami live a nomadic existence. Thus, the question of 'What is an appropriate education for Saami children?' became clearly linked to the importance of reindeer breeding for the national economy. Or as stated in the 1913 school reform, 'a Lapp shall be a Lapp, for then he serves his motherland best'. Swedish educational policy continued, especially with the 1928 Reindeer Pasture Act, wherever possible to keep the Saami children within Saami culture and the nomadic economy (Ruong, 1969b).

Following World War II, the conservationist policy came under heavy attack from Saami seeking greater educational opportunity, and from the Swedish Government which had replaced the Church in the control of Saami schooling. The Swedish Missionary Society's educational efforts then focused almost entirely on the Saami's Folk High School founded during World War II (1942) and located above the Arctic Circle at Jokkmokk after 1945. In this residential 'folk college', Saami youth in their late teens received training in general citizenship, local and national history, reindeer breeding, and other practical subjects. Continuing the 'Lapp will be Lapp' orientation, students were encouraged not to let the two-year course seduce them away from reindeer herding. A policy statement at that time, for example, stressed that:

> Not by following Sweden and things Swedish, but by promoting your mother tongue will you be best fitted to contribute to the common treasures of the fatherland. As Lapps, it is through following your own ways of living and by remaining faithful to your culture that you will keep your place as a part of the Swedish nation. (Ruong, 1969a: 142)

Many young Saami leaving the Saami Folk High School returned to the herding way of life, and a number became leaders in subsequent ethnic organizational development, as in the Swedish Reindeer Herders Association founded in 1950. Others became school teachers and taught Saami children in settled communities and in nomad schools. A third very small group moved into mainstream Swedish society and culture through subsequent professional training. But a number of these assimilated Saami maintained feelings of ethnic solidarity with their Saami origins and a concern for greater social justice in Saami attempts to fend off powerful state and private interests seeking the continued economic exploitation of Lapland's rich natural wealth of minerals, timber, water and scenery (Wallmark, 1958).

Thus, by the 1950s Swedish authorities offered two distinct educational programs for Saami children. For those who lived by reindeer herding, the Nomad Schools, which had become fixed and residential, continued to stress skills and values thought necessary for a nomadic life. For children of the growing number of Saami employed in forestry, agriculture, and fishing, regular primary and, less frequently, secondary schools were built in rural areas — schools taught entirely in Swedish and attended by Swedish youth, schools where the Saami language and culture were viewed as inferior, and where Saami ethnic identity was undesirable and, when possible, to be denied. School failure of Saami children was and is common. In their public school experiences, generations of Saami youth have learned that being a Saami and speaking Saami was strongly associated with defeat, contempt and poverty (With, 1967; Östlund, 1973).

With increasing pressure from the Swedish Social Democratic Government for the acculturation and out-migration of Saami youth, with continued serious infringement of forest and pasture land by 'clear-cutting' forestry practices, by tourism, by mining and water-power development interests, the Saami, a distinct people with thousands of years of traditions as an ethnic community, began to seriously doubt their ability to survive in the early 1950s (Wallmark, 1958; Park, 1959; Otnes, 1970; Lundegård, 1973).

Until recently, upwardly mobile Saami could avoid career defeat only by 'paying' with their identity. One was either a Saami, a Swede, a Norwegian, or a Finn. The few Saami who achieved assimilation, or any Saami for that matter, rarely protested this cost-mechanism (Porsanger, 1965). A few exceptions can be found, mostly among teachers, or isolated individuals who by paying the price had come to know the ideal democratic ideology of the dominant segment, and by simple transfer had come to see the plurification process as an injustice to a cultural minority (Eidheim, 1968). By attempting to point out what might be viewed as a moral injustice according to the dominant group ideology, they jeopardized their careers, were denounced as threats to national security by their superiors, and were generally viewed with alarm by Saami who rightfully feared the consequences of such public role-mixing. Most early Saami critics of existing ethnic relations and internal colonization in Lapland were crushed. A few promoted such non-controversial 'minority activities' as folk arts and crafts in efforts to maintain Saami identity while filling roles reserved to the dominant segment.

Following World War II, a number of important changes at the national and international level created new conditions favorable to efforts of Saami intellectuals with support from individuals and institutions in the dominant segment to create a Saami ethnic movement. This collective effort brought together for the first time those who identified with Saami culture and sought to address serious economic and cultural problems resulting from the position of structured inequality that the Saami had long occupied in the national society. Simultaneously, rapid economic growth and aggressive exploitation of natural resources in traditionally Saami areas had seriously detrimental effects on the herding economy (Svensson, 1970). At the international and national levels, wartime efforts by Nazi Germany to exterminate the Jewish ethnic minority, and strong Scandinavian support for the United Nations' work on human rights, helped to bring the problem of ethnic survival home and to stimulate national debate on the rights and status of under-privileged minorities within the Scandinavian countries (Fimerstad, 1973). Accordingly, the dominant segment became more conscious of supposed injustices in the plurification system, and with support from influential professors, teachers, radical socialists and others, Saami ethnic activists gained a consensus of sorts as to a movement rationale and program (Otnes, 1970; Svensson, 1970).

Since the 1950s the Saami cultural-revival movement has sought to mobilize minority identity through the creation of new organizations that embody the movement's ideology of survival and resistance to acculturation (Eidheim, 1968).

These groups, in turn, have brought pressure on institutions of the dominant society to respond favorably to Saami demands for altered ethnic relations, for a more culturally pluralistic society where Saami cultural survival and Saami participation will be accepted as legitimate national concerns. Saami organizations in the past decade, for example, have called for a number of basic changes in the nine-year comprehensive school that most of their children attend. This reform program places priorities on bilingual instruction in Saami and Swedish during the early grades, the creation of bilingual teacher-training programs, a revised curriculum including Saami history and cultural themes, and a secondary school program especially adapted to the needs of reindeer-herding culture and management.

The conflict of interests that arises from intensifying government efforts to assimilate and incorporate the Saami into the Swedish Welfare State, and Saami efforts to move towards a more autonomous situation in a more culturally pluralistic society are clearly evident in the schools.

Saami students, despite recent special educational arrangements, continue as a group to be under-achievers, withdrawn, and seemingly unable to succeed in national schools. A well-known Saami educator, the Norwegian Anton Hoem, contends that the causes are to be found in competing and conflicting ideologies — i.e. those of the ethnic movement, and those of the national society:

> The investments in special teacher training, textbooks, and literature in Lappish, introduction of Lappish language and culture as subjects are efforts to raise the efficiency of teaching within the established system. They are not efforts to adapt the school to the particular needs and values of Lappish society. Therefore, one will find different standards. In fact, the more efficient the teaching, the greater the discrepancy between goals of education at home and in the school . . . The main results are a cultural and social gap between the most successful pupils and the local Lapp society, and a barrier between losers and the nationwide system. (Hoem, 1968)

Saami movement activists have come to recognize that formal schooling, despite gestures toward bilingual instruction, is essentially about the business of assimilation and social control, and not the strengthening of cultural pluralism. They have, accordingly, in the past few years sought to develop an alternative educational setting where movement ideology could be developed to shape goals, new learning, and action strategies. The Saami Folk High School, a residential school for young adults at Jokkmokk in the Forest Saami area above the Arctic Circle, has begun to carry out this function but only with protracted conflict with the local Commune authorities who reject the legitimacy of 'Saami Power' slogans, the Saami ethnic-revival movement, and the emergence of a Saami-controlled folk school (Lidroth, 1974). Despite local pressures and forceful arguments by a number of Commune leaders to change the school's name and orientation from the Saami Folk High School to something like 'Jokkmokk Commune's FHS', a small core of Saami activists have, during the past several years, used the school to develop an educational strategy seeking to mobilize individual Saami into a politicized ethnic-interest group (Östlund, 1973).

Although the Saami remain a minority on the Folk High School's board of directors and must share control with representatives of the provincial government and the antagonistic local Commune, a number of notable innovations have been secured, albeit with growing animosity between Saami students and the Swedish population both at Jokkmokk and throughout northern Sweden. Studies of how ethnic groups mobilize for political action suggests a number of basic problems that each group must solve (Barth, 1969). These include questions about the distinctiveness of the group, and the need for agreement on standards by which group members can judge themselves and others and determine who lies within the ethnic boundary, and who lies without. These concerns, as well as problems of communication, decision making, authority and the legitimate use of power, of ideology and discipline, and of the indoctrination necessary to keep ideology alive have all been addressed by educational activities at the Saami FHS. Before examining these activities, it may be useful to note that ethnicity has previously been viewed here as a phenomenon useful in the categorization of people. At the folk school, ethnicity has also been a tool employed strategically by movement activists seeking to assist Saami youth to negotiate new individual identities, commitments to struggle, as well as the learning of organizational and communications skills needed to advance the movement's manifest goals of Saami cultural revival and ethnic-minority survival.

Where the Swedish Missionary Society used the Saami Folk High School during the 1940s and 1950s to further the national ethnic policy of socialized isolation, today, Saami activists fight to gain complete control of the school and use it to address their problems and dreams of survival as an ethnic minority in a pluralistic society. Where earlier many of the Reindeer Herders Association leaders had their first training in formal organizational life and social science at the school, today special courses are offered that focus on problems of collective action and minority mobilization. These critical seminars are taught and attended by Saami of different socioeconomic backgrounds and seek to unify the Saami as an ethnic group. Saami from the mountains, the forests, and the cities with differing professions and life-styles meet, discuss, and develop movement ideology and action strategies to strengthen ethnic identification and to gain greater acceptance from a strongly ethnocentric Swedish society.

Courses in the Saami language are also provided and related to the movement's literary and journalistic activities. Classes in Saami history and handicrafts, in reindeer management, and administrative techniques all view Saami culture from perspectives that seek to raise students' consciousness of ethnic membership and the legitimacy of the group's dreams of survival and autonomy. The critical seminars, especially, have frequently been starting points for reformulating the movement's ideological framework, i.e. the 'world view' from which most Saami political actions follow. The joint Nordic Lapp Culture Policy Statement of 1970 entitled, in English, 'We are Lapps and Want to Remain Lapps' clearly indicates efforts in stating the movement's argument and goals (Svenska Samernas Riksförbund, 1971). It is also a document that owes much to the educational and political work of Saami movement activists and supporters at the Saami Folk High School.

The Saami Folk High School today presents an example of an educational institution actively seeking to advance a process of ethnic revival, confrontation arontation and resistance to acculturation that is for the most part viewed unfavorably by members of the dominant society. At the local level, Swedes press for rapid acculturation and incorporation through, if necessary, forced assimilation. At the national level, assimilation is sought instead through a policy of 'tvåkulturell utbildning,' or bicultural education where Swedish and Saami studies will supposedly be given equal value and emphasis (Norrbottenslän, 1968). So far, Saami activists have been largely able to subvert this policy at Jokkmokk and stress the latter. But as this tolerant situation may end at any time, the ethnic movement is pressing for a state-supported rural folk high school under complete Saami control (Östlund, 1973: 287–8).

While most Saami are sympathetic to the movement's broad goals, many express concern about the possible consequences of conflict. One of their older leaders has put it thus: 'We are not a warlike people and we don't fight. Our culture is primitive, and I suppose we have to give in to the stronger one.' Many younger Saami reject the resignation of their elders and, under the rubric of 'Saami Power,' seek to fight back: 'We are not Norwegians, Swedes, or Finns. We are different and we intend to stay that way.' It is this small activist group which seeks to make the Saami Folk High School its own, much to the consternation of many fearful Saami, the Jokkmokk Commune, and the National Board of Education (Lidroth, 1974: Sammallahti, 1975).

Conclusions

It is clear that language maintenance of an ethnic group reinforces the boundaries between that group and the larger society. Boundary maintenance reinforces the ethnic identity of a group and is undertaken for a number of reasons: religious, as in the case of the Amish; politico-economical, as in the case of the French-speaking Canadians; or economic, as in the case of the immigrant American Italian, Slovak, Polish, etc. groups. Often, the major function of language in boundary maintenance is to enable a group to resist assimilation: this is as true of the former superordinate, migrant *Finlands-svenskarna* as it is of the subordinate, indigenous Saami who both use language as a weapon in the fight for ethnic survival.

The degree to which a group becomes bilingual depends partly on the larger society's willingness to let that group assimilate, to grant that group access to the social institutions, and partly on the availability of jobs which require a knowledge of the official language. The Canadian-French immersion programs form a very good example of how job language requirements influence language learning strategies.

Group bilingualism is frequently accompanied by language shift to the official language when there are ample, material rewards in so doing. Institutional enclosure may not be an issue as long as the parallel institutions are open. The French Canadians, who massively shifted to English (and gave cause to the legal measures) in spite of parallel institutions of church, school, recreation, etc., are a case in point. Many migrant superordinate groups do not seem able to maintain their original mother tongue once they are (legally-politically) separated from the home culture as in the case of the Normans and the Franks; probably demographic factors were also at issue. Spanish certainly has been maintained in colonized Latin-America. It is a temptation to claim that language shift takes place when the socio-economical and political rewards of a nation, which are accessible, favor such a shift, but it is likely to be a simplification. It is a claim which is likely to account for the majority of situations of language shift but it will not necessarily account for situations where one would expect language shift but does not find it. It may be that the spatial isolation of the Saami can account for the maintenance of Saami, but it is more likely to be an expression of ethnic identity which will not be surrendered, a mechanism of ethnic boundary maintenance.[3]

Linguists do not have a clear understanding of these issues, and my contention is that in order to understand the nature of bilingualism we need to consider the relationship of these issues. In this paper I have indicated the direction I believe such a discussion should take, but it is very obvious that this paper is only a beginning.

Notes

1. This paper is co-authored in that the Saami case study is written by R. G. Paulston and the rest of the paper by C. B. Paulston. The case study is a much shortened version of the original 'Ethnic revival and education conflict in Swedish Lapland'.

2. The following excerpts are from R. G. Paulston's 'Ethnic revival and educational conflict in Swedish Lapland'. *Comparative Education Review* 20: 2, 179–92. Permission to reprint is gratefully acknowledged.
3. It should be pointed out somewhere that many members of the ethnic groups discussed in this paper do shift languages and assimilate into the larger society, and that this discussion deals with what sometimes amounts to a minority within a minority.

References

BARTH, F. (ed.) 1969, *Ethnic Groups and Boundaries*. Boston: Little, Brown and Company.

BARZUN, J. 1959, *The House of Intellect*. New York: Random House.

BRUDNER, L. 1972, The maintenance of bilingualism in Southern Austria. *Ethnology* 11, 1, 39–54.

EIDHEIM, H. 1968, The Lappish movement: An innovative political process. In M. J. SCHWARTZ (ed.) *Local Level Politics*. Chicago: Aldine.

ELAZAR, D. and FRIEDMAN, M. 1976, *Moving Up: Ethnic Succession in America*. New York: Institute on Pluralism and Group Identity of the American Jewish Committee.

ERICKSON, D. *et al.* 1969, *Community School at Rough Rock — An Evaluation for the Office of Economic Opportunity*. US Department of Commerce. Springfield, Va.: Clearinghouse for Federal Scientific and Technical Information.

FIMERSTAD, L. 1973, Samerna i kolonial situation. *Göteborgs Handels Tidning* August 13.

FISHMAN, J. A. 1966, Language maintenance and language shift as a field of inquiry. *Language Loyalty in the United States*. The Hague: Mouton.

GAARDER, B. n.d., Political perspective on bilingual education. Manuscript. Washington DC: US Office of Education.

GORDON, M. M. 1964, *Assimilation in American Life*. New York: Oxford University Press.

HOEM, A. 1967, *Samenes skolegang*. Oslo: Universitets förlaget.

—— 1968, Samer, skole, og Samfunn. *Tidskrift för Samfunns forskning*.

LIDROTH, B. G. 1974, Norrbotten och dess länsstyrelse samernas största problem. *Norrlandsk Tidskrift* No. 2.

LIEBERSON, S. and CURRY, T. J. 1971, Language shift in the United States: some demographic clues. *International Migration Review* 5, 125–37.

LIEBERSON, S., DALTO, G. and JOHNSTON, M. E. 1975, The course of mother tongue diversity in nations. *American Journal of Sociology* 81, 1, 34–61.

LUNDEGÅRD, M. 1973, Har samekulturen chans överleva. *Dagens Nyheter* December 3.

MASON, M. A. 1976, The educational programs and activities of the Black Panther Party (1966–1971): An analysis and assessment. Manuscript. Pittsburgh: University of Pittsburgh, International and Development Education Program.

MOHAMMAD, W. E. 1976, *The Man and the Woman in Islam*. Chicago: The Hon. Elijah Mohammad Mosque No. 2.

NEWTON, H. P. 1972, *To Die for the People: The Writings of Huey P. Newton*. New York: Random House.

NORDBERG, E. 1956, Arjeplogs Lappskola. *Årsböcker i svensk undervisnings-historia* Vol. 89/90.

NORRBOTTENSLÄN 1968, *The Teaching of Lapps.* Luleå: Board of Education.

ÖSTLUND, B. 1973, Samernas folkhögskola och samerna. *Tidskrift för svenska folkhögskolan* 54.

OTNES, P. 1970, *Den samiske nasjon: Interresseorganisasjoner i samenes politiske historie.* Oslo: Pax Förlag.

PARK, G. 1959, Samernas framtid: ett svenskt dilemma. *Samefolkets Egen Tidning* 41, 19–23.

PAULSTON, C. B. 1975a, *Implications of Language Learning Theory for Language Planning.* Arlington, Va.: Center for Applied Linguistics.

—— 1975b, Ethnic relations and bilingual education: accounting for contradictory data. In R. C. TROIKE and N. MODIANO (eds) *Proceedings of the First Inter-American Conference on Bilingual Education.* Washington, DC: Center for Applied Linguistics.

—— 1977, Tvåspråkig utbildning i USA, 1976. *Invandrare och Minoriteter* No. 5.

PAULSTON, R. G. 1972, Cultural revitalization and educational change in Cuba. *Comparative Education Review* 16, 3, 474–85.

—— 1976a, Ethnic revival and educational conflict in Swedish Lapland. *Comparative Education Review* 20, 2, 179–92.

—— 1976b, Separate education as an ethnic survival strategy: the Finlandssvenska case. Manuscript.

—— 1976c, Ethnicity and educational change: a research priority for comparative education. *Comparative Education Review* 20, 3.

PORSANGER, S. 1965, The sense of solidarity among the Lapps. *Studia Ethnographica Upsaliensis* 21.

RUONG, I. 1969a, *Samerna.* Stockholm: Bonniers.

—— 1969b, Views about the Lapps. In R. G. P. HILL and K. NICUL (eds) *The Lapps Today* Vol. 2. Oslo: Universitets förlaget.

SAMMALLAHTI, P. 1975, Samernas språk och skolförhållanden i Finland. *Nordisk Minoritets forskning* 2.

SCHERMERHORN, R. A. 1970, *Comparative Ethnic Relations: A Framework for Theory and Research.* New York: Random House.

—— 1972, Towards a general theory of minority groups. Cited in A. VERDOODT (1972: 379 ff.).

SKUTNABB-KANGAS, T. 1975, Om finnarnas svårigheter i att förstå danska. *Spåk i Norden.*

Svenska Samernas Riksförbund 1971, *Protokoll, samernas same politiska program.* Stockholm: The Association.

SVENSSON, T. G. 1970, Economic modernization and conflict. *Ethnograhic Museum: University of Oslo Yearbook, 1970.* Oslo: Universitetsförlaget.

THOMPSON, R. M. 1974, Mexican American language loyalty and the validity of the 1970 Census. *International Journal of the Sociology of Language* 2, 6–18.

VERDOODT, A. 1972, The differential impact of immigrant French speakers on indigenous German speakers: a case study in the light of two theories. In J. FISHMAN (ed.) *Advances in the Sociology of Language,* Part II. The Hague: Mouton.

WALLACE, A. 1956, Revitalization movements. *American Anthropologist* 58, 264–81.

—— 1975, Schools in revolutionary and conservative societies. In F. A. J. IANNI (ed.) *Conflict and Change in Education*. Glenview, Ill.: Scott, Foresman and Company,

WALLMARK, L. 1958, Är Sveriges samer dömda att försvinna? *Bland Sveriges Samer*. Stockholm.

WITH, T. 1967, Noen refleksjoner. *Sami Aellin 1953–1955*. Oslo.

YODER, C. 1976, Diglossia within the Old Order Amish speech community of Lancaster, Pennsylvania. Manuscript. University of Pittsburgh, Department of General Linguistics.

4 Theoretical Perspectives on Bilingual Education Programs

In this paper, the main questions I would like to address are as follows:

(1) What are the key independent variables or causal factors which influence bilingual education programs?[1]
(2) What are the key dependent variables or outcomes of bilingual education programs?
(3) What are some of the major intervening variables or factors modifying such outcomes.

Introduction

The major point of this paper is that there is no single answer to these questions, but rather that the identification of the independent variables, and the interpretation of outcomes depend on the worldview of the researcher and the particular theory she/he employs to explain and predict phenomena. In this paper I will attempt to outline some major theories of social and educational change and to delineate the identification and interpretation of variables of bilingual education within the framework of each particular theory. In so doing, I am drawing heavily on the work by R. G. Paulston (1976) in his *Conflicting Theories of Social and Educational Change: A Typological Review*.

We can probably all agree on the basic phenomena which form the background to Title VII bilingual education programs in the United States and which gave rise to the original legislation of Title VII: there are a number of children from a low socioeconomic status (SES) background who speak no or poor English and who encounter massive school failure with consequent early school drop out and low integration into the economic life of the nation. It is when we consider why this is so, what treatment these children should be accorded, and what outcomes should follow that considerable disagreement ensues. Such scholarly disagreement at times becomes public and divisive.

Although other fields of study have looked at scholarly strife within their disciplines from the notion of Kuhn's (1971) paradigm shift, I know of no attempt to understand the dimensions of bilingual education from a conceptual framework of paradigms. By paradigms, Kuhn means 'the way a scientific/professional community views a field of study, identifies appropriate problems for study, and specifies legitimate concepts and methods'. He contends that:

> Men whose research is based on shared paradigms are committed to the same rules and standards . . . and continuation of a particular research tradition . . . paradigm is a criterion for choosing problems that, while the paradigm is taken for granted, can be assumed to have solutions. To a great extent, these are the only problems that the community will admit as scientific or encourage its members to undertake. A paradigm can even isolate the community from those socially important problems that are not reducible to puzzle form, because they cannot be stated in terms of the conceptual and instrumental tools the paradigm supplies. (Kuhn cited in R. G. Paulston, 1976: 5)

In other words, it is only through an examination of the various theoretical frameworks used to explain and predict the phenomena of bilingual education that we can put into perspective the conflicting or at times complementary research questions and the anticipated solutions as they relate to the dimensions of bilingual education.

R. G. Paulston, drawing on the literature of social and educational change, posits two major paradigms: the functional or 'equilibrium' paradigm and the conflict paradigm. Theories (which admittedly cross and overlap) that fall within the 'equilibrium' paradigm are evolutionary and neo-evolutionary, structural-functionalist, and system analysis. Basically these theories are all concerned with maintaining society in an equilibrium through the harmonious relationship of the social components and they emphasize smooth, cumulative change. Theoretical approaches which fall within the conflict paradigm are group conflict theory, cultural revitalization theory, and an anarchistic-utopian approach. 'Theories which cluster more or less within the conflict paradigm emphasize the inherent instability of social systems and the conflicts over values, resources, and power that follow as a natural consequence' (R. G. Paulston, 1976: 7). Major issues are economic conflict, conflicting value and cultural systems, and conflict arising from oppressive institutions and imperfect human nature.

Assuredly, all of these theoretical approaches are not equally represented in the attempts to delimit and comprehend the dimensions of bilingual education. Nevertheless, it is instructive to examine studies typical of each approach for their underlying assumptions, basic questions, and putative solutions in order to illustrate the basic premise of the paper, namely that each theory will identify differently the key variables and their relationship, and consequently the answers they seek will differ. Even at times when the question remains the same, the goals and the means to those goals will vary according to the theoretical approach. For the purpose of illustration, I have identified a number of studies which most clearly exemplify a particular approach. Granted, a number of studies incorporate aspects from more than one theoretical framework, and on the whole I have tended to avoid such studies. Furthermore, a very large amount of studies on bilingual education is purely descriptive and atheoretical; such studies I have ignored. It is readily seen then that this paper does not intend a review of the literature (for that, see Engle, 1975; Fishman, 1976; C. B. Paulston, 1976b) but rather a selective analysis of a few template works.

The Equilibrium Paradigm

Evolutionary theory

Classical evolutionary theories are strongly influenced by Darwin's work on biological evolution and seek sociological analogues to the living organism (L. Ward, 1904; Parsons, 1964). They are characterized by notions of progress, by stages of development from lower- to higher-order forms. Society is viewed as an organism with specialized structures facilitating survival. Education, as an 'integrative' structure, functions to maintain stability and changes from 'simple' or 'primitive' forms to more complex 'modern' forms in response to change in other structures. Thus as societies 'progress' or become increasingly differentiated (here the evolutionists borrow the biologists' exact terminology), educational systems come under increasing pressure to specialize and adapt. (R. G. Paulston, 1976: 7)

The only theoretical approach relating to bilingual education which falls in the evolutionary category is the genetic theories of Jensen (1969), Herrnstein (1971), and others. In short, the geneticists account for the lack of school achievement by students from minority groups, as well as by those from lower SES background, on the ground of these students' hereditary inferior intelligence quotients (IQ). Few issues so well illustrate the paradigm clash as the debate over IQ and to illustrate, I would like to draw at length on Bowles, Gintis & Meyer's (1975–6) critique, written from a group conflict perspective, of both Jensen and his colleagues and of the structural functionalists' position on this issue.

In 'Education, IQ, and the legitimation of the social division of labor', Bowles, Gintis & Meyer consider the educational system in the United States as a mechanism for the reproduction of the social division of labor and focus their inquiry on the legitimation of this division and on the process of assigning individuals to its various positions. 'We say that a social process is *legitimated* when individuals are sufficiently convinced of its inevitability, desirability, or justness that united class action towards the transformation of the process is rendered infeasible' (Bowles, Gintis & Meyer, 1975–6: 234). They examine this legitimation function within what they label techno-cratic-meritocratic ideology which, as they define it, corresponds fairly closely to the structural-functionalist position:

> The educational system legitimates economic inequality by providing an ostensibly open, objective and meritocratic mechanism for assigning individuals to unequal economic positions. Indeed, the more meritocratic the educational process appears, the better it serves to legitimate inequality. For the educational system fosters and reinforces the belief that economic success depends on the possession of technical and cognitive skills — skills which it is organized to provide in an efficient, equitable and unbiased manner on the basis of the meritocratic principle. (Bowles, Gintis & Meyer, 1975–6: 234)

They cite (p. 237) the conclusion that David & Moore reach in their highly influential 'functional theory of stratification': 'Social inequality is thus an unconsciously evolved device by which societies insure that the most important positions are conscientiously filled by the most qualified persons' (David & Moore in Bendix & Lipset, 1966). Bowles, Gintis & Meyer go on to argue against such an interpretation: educational tracking based on competitive grading and objective test scores is only tangentially related to social efficiency. Nowhere are the notions of meritocracy seen more clearly, they continue, than in the recent IQ debate between the geneticists and the structural-functionalists where it is assumed that IQ is an important indicator of economic success, an assumption the authors consider faulty.

The authors point out that the major periods of liberal educational reform have been marked by a lack of concern with genetically inherited characteristics when the major problem rather was perceived to be one of structuring an environment that would promote rather than retard individual growth. 'Yet the demise of each liberal reform movement has been greeted by a genetic backlash: if improving the school environment does not achieve its elevated objectives, there must be something wrong with the kids' (Bowles, Gintis & Meyer, 1975–6: 249).

And so Jensen argued in 1969 that the failure of compensatory education to raise scholastic achievement levels must be due to the heritability of IQ.[2]

> The assertions of Jensen, Herrnstein and others constituted a fundamental attack on the liberal reformist position. Yet the defense has been curiously superficial: the putative economic importance of IQ has remained undocumented by the genetic school and unchallenged by the environmentalists . . . not one of their environmentalist critics has taken the economic importance of IQ any less for granted. (Bowles, Gintis & Meyer, 1975–6: 250)

Bowles, Gintis & Meyer, on the other hand, claim, on the basis of their empirical data, that IQ is not an important cause of economic success and that 'the intense debate on the heritability of IQ is thus largely irrelevant to an understanding of poverty, wealth, and inequality of opportunity in the United States' (p. 251). They go on to point out that the modern liberal approach is to attribute social class differences to unequal opportunity, i.e. the failures and successes of parents are passed onto their children via distinct learning and cultural environments. 'The achievement of a more equal society merely requires that all youth be afforded the educational and other social conditions of the best and most successful' (p. 254), an assumption reminiscent of that behind Title VII. The liberals don't deal with IQ differences among whites (which the authors seem to accept) of different social class backgrounds, nor do they question the causal role of IQ in getting ahead economically.

> Thus the proposition, adhered to by present day conservatives and liberals of past generations, that social classes sort themselves out on the basis of innate individual capacity to cope successfully in the social environment, and hence tend to reproduce themselves from generation to generation, is restored. (Bowles, Gintis & Meyer, 1975–6: 255)

The authors conclude by presenting data to support their major proposition: 'the fact that economic success tends to run in the family arises almost completely independently from any inheritance of IQ; genetic or environmental' (p. 258). 'The power and privilege of the capitalist class are often inherited, but not through superior genes' (p. 263). In other words, high SES is transmitted to the children of parents of high SES, and one mechanism of this transmittance is the school system.

We see then, on this particular issue, that although the three approaches, evolutionary (genetic school); structural-functionalist (technico-merito-cratic liberals); and group conflict (Bowles, Gintis & Meyer), recognize the same basic variables, they perceive a very different relationship between these same variables and, as well, their underlying assumptions vary widely.

The chart in Table 4.1 may help clarify this point.

TABLE 4.1 *Variables and their relationship in three theoretical approaches*

Approach	Variables:		
	Independent	Intervening	Dependent
EQUILIBRIUM:			
A. Evolutionary	IQ	Scholastic success	Economic success SES
	Assumption:	*IQ hereditary*	
B. Structural-functionalist	IQ/Merit	Function of school to select according to merit in division of labor	Economic success SES
	Assumption:	*IQ by nurture (unequal opportunity); schools give equal chance to meritorious students*	
CONFLICT			
Group conflict	SES	Function of school to legitimize (unequally) division of labor	Economic success or lack of
	Assumption:	*IQ heriditary but irrelevant as a variable; schools function in the interest of the elites*	

Structural-functional theory

Although the structural-functional, or S/F, framework is a discrete set of interrelated assumptions about values, norms, and appropriate questions and methods, it is to a considerable degree a twentieth-century version of evolutionary theory. But where the evolutionists placed primary emphasis on linked stages of socioeconomic and cultural development, the S/F theorists focus on the homeostatic or balancing mechanisms by which societies maintain a 'uniform state'. Both theories view societies as essentially stable yet highly complex and differentiated. As the values embodied in institutions such as the educational sub-system are viewed as extremely durable, boundary exchanges between the sub-system and the environment will be equilibrating, i.e. they will tend toward balance. (R. G. Paulston, 1976: 13)

Structural-functional theory, as exemplified by Merton (1957), Homans (1950), and Parsons (1951) (Larkin, 1970), has been the dominant theory of social change in American social sciences and has had a strong influence on the interpretation of educational systems and valid educational reform. I don't think that it is an exaggeration to say that the majority of writings on bilingual education fall under this category as I shall attempt to illustrate. This approach tends to be the position (almost always tacitly assumed) of the ESL proponents in the ESL versus BE controversy. And it is most certainly the position of the US government.

In the Bilingual Education Act, Congress recognizes the problems of limited English-speaking children from low income families and spells out the measures to be taken in order to cope with these problems:

. . . the Congress declares it to be the policy of the United States, in order to establish equal educational opportunity for all children (A) to encourage the establishment and operation, where appropriate, of educational programs using bilingual educational practices, techniques, and methods, and (B) . . . to provide financial assistance to . . . educational agencies . . . in order to . . . develop and carry out such programs, . . . which are designed to meet the educational needs of such children; and of demonstrating effective ways of providing, for children of limited English-speaking ability, instruction designed to enable them, while using their native language, to achieve competence in the English language. (Geffert *et al.*, 1975: 13)

The assumptions are clearly recognizable:

(1) the lack of social and economic success on the part of these minority groups is due to (a) 'unequal opportunity' (cf. Bowles & Gintis, 1975) as

manifest through different language, different culture, and different learning styles,[3] and (b) to a lack of scholastic success as a group[4] because of poor English-speaking ability;

(2) with the provision of English skills, merit and IQ will lead through scholastic skills gained in a 'meaningful education' to social and economic success.

The immediate objective of bilingual education programs is then given: to equalize opportunity for children from limited English-speaking families by compensatory training in English where such training can be theoretically interpreted as a balancing mechanism to maintain the equilibrium of society, as in this approach 'intra-system conflict is usually viewed as pathological, as an indicator of systemic breakdown' (R. G. Paulston, 1976: 13). Larkin (1970: 113), writing from a structural-functional perspective, points out that in a technological society such as ours, 'equilibrium is maintained by the educational institution', whose major function is seen as the socialization of youth. According to Larkin, the socialization process is two dimensional. The instrumental aspect is the provision of technical competence: education is to provide the students with salable skills (of which, for our purposes, English language proficiency can be seen as the major skill). The expressive aspect is a 'normative orientation in harmony with the values of society' (Larkin, 1970: 113), or in the terminology more frequently found in the literature on bilingual education, facilitating assimilation into the dominant, mainstream culture. But to the S/F theorists, the value transmission function of the schools serves a wider purpose than just assimilation, namely that of 'pattern maintenance,' in Parsons' terms:

> According to Parsons, provision for pattern maintenance is a functional prerequisite of all societies:
>
>> . . . the social system . . . depends on the requisite minimum of 'support' from each of the other systems. It must, that is, have a sufficient proportion of its component actors adequately motivated to act in accordance with the requirements of its role-system, positively in abstention from too much disruptive, i.e. deviant, behavior (Parsons, 1959: 27).
>
> The expressive aspect of the socialization process is socialization of youth to a social order by instilling values necessary for the continuation of the social system. (Larkin, 1970: 113)

While this view of the function of schools is reminiscent of Bowles & Gintis' (1975) legitimation process, the two approaches differ profoundly in their attitude toward such a process. The S/F proponents see this process as highly functional in ensuring that the most qualified persons fill the most important positions, and they 'contend that inequality is not only inevitable, but necessary and beneficial to all since individual survival is contingent on the survival and well-being of society' (R. G. Paulston, 1976: 13). Parsons no doubt would consider Bowles & Gintis' viewpoint as 'too much disruptive'. The latter would be likely to agree with Hill-Burnett that:

> The key to access to a position is not the competence of the performer but the answer to the question of who has authority to judge whether the performance meets the standards, and to the question of how the judge is linked to the other arrangements in the society for maintaining a given constellation of differentiated resources and power over resources. (Hill-Burnett, 1976: 37)

One is reminded of the debate in bilingual education over teacher training and competencies. The major issues, on the surface, seem to be language proficiency in the L1 (mother tongue, here minority vernacular) and L2 (target language, here English) and professional educational training in order to meet State requirements for teacher certification. But the question of proficiency masks the real question which concerns ethnic group membership; is the teacher Anglo or member of the L1 ethnic group? Bilingual education proponents typically claim that teachers should be members of the same cultural group as the students and tend to ignore the teachers' proficiency in English as an important qualification. Their position, whether theoretical or not, tends to be one of conflict orientation, frequently tending toward utopian ideology. ESL (English as a Second Language) proponents, on the other hand, typically insist on discussing issues at the level of method and technique, a characteristic of the S/F approach. They see fluency in English and a thorough training in the techniques of ESL as the major requirement amongst the competencies of a teacher of limited English-speaking children. They tend to exemplify Larkin's points that (1) innovation is threatening as it temporarily upsets the equilibrium, and (2) any pressure for change will be met by resistance from those office holders who have vested interests.

Access to teaching jobs in bilingual education programs becomes very much a question of 'who has the authority to judge whether the performance meets the standards?' The standards of course are determined by the perceived goals of bilingual education. The US government and its legislators officially conceive of the goal of bilingual education as assimilation of minority group members through transitional bilingual education programs where the emphasis can be interpreted from the viewpoint of S/F theory as maintaining vertical equilibrium 'by translation of societal needs and goals into institutional goals. In turn, the institutions must be organized to efficiently and effectively implement these goals and satisfy societal needs' (Larkin, 1970: 113).

Efficiently and *effectively* are indeed the key terms for the major concerns of the research on bilingual education from an S/F perspective. As an ERIC search will quickly demonstrate, there is a pervasive technocratic concern with methods, techniques, curriculum and teacher training, no doubt partially because these types of projects tend to get funded by the Office of Education. After a perusal of the literature on bilingual education as found in ERIC or in doctoral dissertations, one cannot avoid coming away with a vague feeling that the most important objectives of these programs are for the children to increase their standardized scores on tests in language arts, mathematics and self concept; to demonstrate that teaching in the mother tongue results in the more efficient learning of English.

While the research, whether of equilibrium or conflict theory orientation, which R. G. Paulston discusses is concerned primarily with social or educational change at the national level (Parsons' (1961) societal and institutional levels), the majority of research and writing on bilingual education, especially recent work in North America, tends to be at the programmatic-operational level. The research typical of the S/F approach usually treats the bilingual education programs as the independent variable, as the causal factor which accounts for certain subsequent results, for certain behaviors in children. One problem with such research is that these studies carry in and of themselves virtually no generalizability to other programs, as Mackey (1972) and Macnamara (1972) are careful to point out. Nowhere is this problem seen more clearly than in a comparison of the S/F oriented research on the Title VII Bilingual Education programs in the United States with the research on the immersion programs in Canada. Many descriptions and comparisons of these programs exist (Andersson & Boyer, 1970; Cohen & Swain, 1976; John & Horner, 1971; C. B. Paulston, 1975b, 1976b; Swain, 1972; Swain & Bruck, 1976; US Commission on Civil Rights, 1975; etc.) and need not be repeated here. Basically, the Title VII programs are for lower-class children from socially stigmatized ethnic minority groups; the immersion programs are for middle-class children from the Anglo majority, a group in social and economic power.

On the surface, both sets of studies show great similarity in research designs: both sets treat instruction as the independent variable; both sets tend to recognize IQ, age and sex as intervening variables and, when feasible, match or control for these variables. Presumably the researchers also recognize the importance of merit (personality factors such as industry, perseverence, motivation, etc.), but as a formal variable in research design, merit tends to be ignored, and indeed Swain (1976a) laments that the kind of psychometric data these studies collect masks individual achievement. The major dependent variable or program outcome for both sets of studies is scholastic skills, primarily proficiency in the two languages (as measured by standardized tests in language arts) and in mathematics. Other additional dependent variables like cognitive development and self-concept can be found in many studies.

Because of their similarity of research design, of identically labelled variables in the same basic relationship, generalizations are frequently made from one set of studies to the other or to be exact, from the Canadian studies to the US children and to other minority group children as well. I have said elsewhere that I consider the St Lambert study (Lambert & Tucker, 1972) one of the most potentially dangerous studies I know as its findings are so often cited as a rationale *against* bilingual education for minority group members. It is important therefore to examine how these studies differ, even though they share the same basic S/F perspective, in their initial motivation, in the selection of relevant assumptions and in long-range goals. The fact that these issues are rarely made explicit nor discussed in these studies can be considered as an S/F characteristic to minimize, if not avoid, intra-system conflict, as an attempt to seek a balancing mechanism to maintain a uniform state through adaptive change.

Although both the US and the Canadian studies are concerned with language proficiency in the L1 and L2, the interest in L2 acquisition and proficiency stems from a widely disparate motivation. The US studies attempt to demonstrate that children who are first taught to read in the L1 will eventually read better in the L2 than similar children in monolingual English programs and also that these children will achieve a higher proficiency in the L2 through the medium of their mother tongue than children who go directly into an L2 curriculum (submersion programs in Lambert's terms; for a discussion of the difference between immersion and submersion programs, see Cohen & Swain, 1976). The Canadian studies, on the other hand, undertake to demonstrate that initial reading in the L2 (i.e. initial literacy) will have no negative consequences on either later reading or language arts skills in the L1; they also seek to demonstrate that the L2 proficiency of the children in immersion programs is superior to that found in traditional programs.

Not surprisingly, different assumptions motivate the undertaking of the two sets of research studies. These assumptions are rarely spelled out explicitly as assumptions but are rather accepted axiomatically or tacitly taken for granted. We need therefore to examine these assumptions — and the long-range goals — of the two sets of studies in order to better be able to interpret and maybe even generalize from the research findings.

The major basic assumption which underlies the US Title VII programs is that of 'unequal opportunity' and the belief that bilingual education helps equalize such shortcomings of opportunity. Andersson & Boyer (1970: 144) outline some long-range implications for society:

> . . . so national expansion of bilingual schooling has certain implications for society as a whole. As suggestive of others, we mention the following: . . . A concern by all Americans for the elimination of poverty, based on the realization that the educational improvement of the poor (which include many speakers of other languages who are presently handicapped in English) helps to raise the socioeconomic level of the population. A higher income level can in turn benefit education, setting an upward spiral. (Andersson & Boyer, 1970: 144)

They continue by looking at the experience of foreign aid:

> Jacoby defines 'development' as 'a complex socio-political-economic process whereby a people of a country progress from a static traditional mode of life toward a modern dynamic society (1969: 5). The similarities between this complex problem and the educational problem with which we are concerned in this book are striking. (Andersson & Boyer, 1970: 145)

Such statements are the hallmark of the liberal structural-functional position. Poor people from traditional ways of life will *progress* (cf. the evolutionist position) to higher socioeconomic levels through educational improvement. These assumptions are echoed by the United States Commission on Civil Rights:

> Following is a discussion of how bilingual bicultural education provides equal educational opportunity. Emphasis is placed on the most important elements in any educational program: fostering self concept and developing cognition, language expression, reading, and English skills. (US Commission on Civil Rights, 1975: 30)

We have a Supreme Court ruling that equal educational opportunity implies partial education in the mother tongue. Similar to the unquestioned relationship between IQ and economic success which Bowles & Gintis (1975) discuss, I know of no research which investigates whether equal educational opportunity as manifest through bilingual education programs really leads to raised socioeconomic status. It is the major assumption of bilingual education, but among structural-functional research it remains not only untested but also unquestioned — it is a question outside the paradigm.

The second major assumption is the importance of the culture contact situation in the schools. The very definition of bilingual education (see Note 1) acknowledges the importance of the mother tongue culture: 'Bilingual education . . . includes the study of the history and culture associated with the mother tongue . . . a legitimate pride in both cultures.' From this assumption follows the emphasis that the teacher be from the same ethnic background as the children: 'One way bilingual bicultural education further enhances self concept is by utilizing language minority teachers to reinforce the child's background and culture' (US Commission on Civil Rights, 1975: 39). Consequently, the ethnic identity of the teacher is occasionally a sub-variable under the independent variable *instruction*.

From this assumption as well follows the interest in what is commonly called cross-cultural communication (although the focus often is on mis-communication). Other closely similar areas of interest and investigation include communicative competence (Hymes, 1972: C. B. Paulston, 1974), socio-linguistic competence (Ervin-Tripp, 1973: 293), interactional com-petence (Mehan, 1972) and social interaction (Grimshaw, 1973), all of which have in common the focus on the social meaning of language, on the social rules of language use, 'the systemic sets of social interactional rules' in Grimshaw's (1973: 109) terms. Although most research on symbolic inter-action (Goffman, 1959, 1961; Garfinkel, 1967; Cicourel, 1970) in bilingual programs is written from a conflict perspective, there is found in many S/F studies a concern, though rarely studied systematically, that teachers may misinterpret their minority students' behavior because of contrasting interactional rules as in, e.g. the use of space, eye contact, voice level, etc. and in permitted speech acts, like types of questions. There is also the con-cern voiced that Anglo teachers may allow any kind of aberrant behavior from minority students out of misplaced cultural tolerance because they don't know what the acceptable norms are.

Future research is likely to give increased importance to the area of communicative competence because it not only is of interest to those whose primary concern lies in the interaction between members of different cul-tures, but also holds significance for theoretical issues in language acquisi-tion. A current assumption about L2 acquisition is that language must be used for purposes of communication if it is to be well learnt, and a number of classroom techniques have been worked out which incorporate social interactional rules of the L2 into classroom practices (Applegate, 1975;

Holmes & Brown, 1976; Jacobson, 1976; C. B. Paulston, 1976a; White, 1974).

One elusive assumption of US bilingual programs is that one method will eventually be found to be more effective than others, and studies occasionally incorporate *method* as well as *medium* under the independent variable *instruction*. We know surprisingly little about methods of language teaching in elementary bilingual programs compared with what we know about methods of teaching adults. Because of the S/F definition of the problem as one of limited English speaking ability and of the perceived treatment as one of instruction, there is a pervasive tendency to look for solutions to problems *within* the programs, and future research is most likely to investigate methods of bilingual instruction more carefully than in the past, where medium of instruction has been the major variable of *instruction*.

Two less influential assumptions remain. S/F research tends to take for granted that ability and merit influence the attainment of scholastic skills and that once equal opportunity has been provided for by bilingual education, such ability will result in success in school. Research designs therefore tend to neutralize such causal influence on the findings by treating IQ, age, and sex (sex is subsumed under merit as girls are perceived to be stronger motivated, harder working, etc.) as intervening variables and where possible control for such influence by matching groups or by statistical techniques.

The other assumption holds that there is some relationship between language and cognition. Language is believed to be the 'vehicle for complex thinking' (Finocchiaro & King, 1966) and the necessity to use the language the children know best then becomes axiomatic (US Commission on Civil Rights, 1975: 44). But the section on *Cognitive and Language Development* (pp. 41–7) is characteristic of other writings on this topic in bilingual education; it contains not one single reference to empirical work on cognitive development of children in bilingual programs. This topic remains poorly explored in these studies; the Scandinavian studies, the majority of which are in the S/F approach, are in sharp contrast with their exploration of the possible consequences of semilingualism on cognitive development (Loman, 1974; Skutnabb-Kangas & Toukomaa, 1976). My personal suspicion is that the question of language and cognition is perceived by many researchers as being outside the paradigm. The earlier studies (Darcy, 1953) on bilingualism and IQ still rankle, and the topic of language and cognition is frequently dismissed with vague comments on the invalidity of the instruments used in such research.

To sum up, the S/F research on bilingual education in the United States is characterized by two major assumptions, 'unequal opportunity' and 'cultural diversity' and I have attempted to show how these assumptions contribute to give structure to the research studies. Two additional factors which influence the research are: (1) the majority of researchers on bilingual education are either educators or social scientists drawing, in contrast to the Canadians, primarily on linguistics, anthropology, and sociology, and (2) the perceived long-range goals are those of harmonious integration into the larger society by equalizing opportunity.

The Canadian immersion programs (see Swain, 1976b, for a bibliography) are very different from the Title VII programs. The long-range goals of the immersion programs especially outside of Quebec, as perceived by most parents, are maintenance of the family SES *quo,* and, because of Canadian legislation *vis à vis* language, they see bilingualism in French/ English as a necessary condition for their children to compete successfully in the job market. There were other motivations as well:

> Some members of the group had generally more 'instrumental' reasons for wishing their children to be bilingual. They wished the continuing progress and success of their children in a province progressively becoming more dominated by the French fact. Others considered bilingualism a personal asset for cultural, intellectual, and social reasons — the so-called 'integrative' motivation. All were concerned with French–English relations in the province, at a time when these were not yet making the headlines. (Melikoff, 1972: 221)

The Canadian researchers, the majority of whom are psychologists, have tended to slight social factors in their research and to minimize the potential conflict situation between the English- and French-speaking groups, but they do acknowledge that '(t)here is no doubt that the language policy at both the federal and provincial levels of Canadian government is helping to provide incentive for English-Canadian parents to enroll their children in French immersion programs' (Cohen & Swain, 1976: 49).

From the difference in long-range goals follows the difference in the underlying assumptions. Since the children in the immersion programs come from the socially and economically dominant Anglo group (Lieberson, 1970), who has managed perfectly well in the English-medium schools, all notions of 'unequal opportunity' become simply irrelevant.

Similarly, the notions of 'cultural diversity' are irrelevant. No one is concerned that Anglo ideo-cultural behavior might become stigmatized and held against the children by their teachers. The Anglo parents, children, and researchers take their own culture for granted, and in the Canadian literature there is no counterpart to the writings on ethnic minority groups' culture and behavior in the schools which we find in the United States (Pialorsi, 1974; Turner, 1973). The programs are housed in Anglo schools and, in fact, the children in class function in French with the communicative competence of English, i.e. they are not expected to give up their social interactional ways of speaking, their cultural ways of being:

> As a trivial example, in a class I visited, in answer to a question from the teacher the children waved their hands and shouted *je sais, je sais* (in direct translation from English in the sense of, please call on me). A French Canadian child would have said *moi, moi* as Guy Dumas pointed out to me later. The children were not corrected. (C. B. Paulston, 1976b: 20)

Nor is there any emphasis on the target culture to compare with that which we find in the United States. The definition of bilingual education in *Bilingual Schooling* (Swain, 1972) contrasts clearly with the American in that there is no mention of culture:

> Bilingual education can be defined as schooling provided fully or partly in a second language with the object in view of making students proficient in the second language while, at the same time, maintaining and developing their proficiency in the first language and fully guaranteeing their education development. (Stern, 1972: 1)

Nowhere is this perceived irrelevance of 'cultural diversity' seen more clearly than in the teacher variable. As we saw in the Title VII studies, the ethnic membership of the teacher is occasionally included as a variable under *instruction*; I don't know of a single Canadian study of the immersion programs that investigates teacher ethnicity as a variable. One reason is that there is no concern about the teacher's cultural background as long as s/he is a fluent speaker of French; the majority of classrooms I have visited have had non-native Canadians as teachers: Belgian, Moroccan, French, etc. rather than French Canadians. In fact, the speech of French-Canadians is occasionally criticized; to illustrate, after a classroom visit, I recall my colleague disdaining the use of the calque *attaque de coeur* instead of the 'proper' *crise cardiaque* and, worse, the use of a masculine adjectival *-al* suffix in the plural. Clearly, the program goal is linguistic competence in standard French, not communicative competence in Canadian French. It hardly needs be added that none of these issues are tapped in the formal research designs.

The Anglo-Canadians do expect the children to show enhanced cultural tolerance-understanding for the Franco-Canadians through the increasing knowledge of French. I don't know of any research which tries to establish that a knowledge of French does *not* result in increased liking for French Canadians[5] — such a question is outside the paradigm; the emphasis is on the harmonious balanced whole. The only one to question the relationship between French proficiency and French culture-tolerance is the usual *bête noire* Macnamara (whose work I make no attempt to type):

> And the average English Canadian's understanding of French Canadians will have to become a lot deeper and less bigoted than it is at present . . . It is unlikely that the mutual trust, sympathy, understanding, and friendship of the two linguistic groups will be achieved by schools alone . . . This probably dooms the enterprise to failure. It may even be more sinister. It may tend to exploit the weakest sector of society, the sector least likely to resist. (Macnamara, 1972: 8)

This quotation from Macnamara serves as a clear contrast; his assumptions are in profound opposition to those characteristic of the S/F approach.

The formal research primarily seeks to tap the implications which follow from the major assumption underlying the immersion programs: a second language can be learned fluently in the school only if it is used as a medium of instruction, as a means to an end, rather than studied as a subject, as an end in itself. Consequently, the children are taught from the beginning in the L2 in language art skills programs similar to those for native speaking children. The extensive testing, primarily by means of standardized tests, which is basically what the immersion research consists of, was undertaken to assure parents (the programs are voluntary) and administrators that the immersion programs work.

> There is no question at all about the efficacy of the Canadian immersion programs, and if anything, the amazing dexterity and charm of the children as they negotiate in French get lost in the published data. (C. B. Paulston, 1976b: 20; see also e.g. the St Lambert study on the proto-type program, Lambert & Tucker, 1972)

We see then that although the US and Canadian research studies are similar in that they see *instruction,* especially *medium of,* as the independent variable and scholastic skills as the dependent variable, they vary in the order of introducing medium of instruction so that the Canadian programs reverse the order of the American L1 → L2 to L2 → L1. The Canadian programs eschew the ESL approach, i.e. here FSL (French as a Second Language) techniques, in favor of basic language arts training[6] and consider cultural diversity as an irrelevant variable; consequently neither *method* nor *teacher* appears as a design variable in the Canadian studies.

We also find the familiar assumptions of a relationship between language and (1) cognition and (2) IQ, age, and sex. In my opinion, the Canadian studies are much more interesting than the American in their work on language and cognition, presumably, I should imagine, because the researchers are not unduly worried about adverse results. Cummins' work is especially worth citing. He speculates in 'The influence of bilingualism on cognitive growth: a synthesis of research findings and explanatory hypothesis' (Cummins, 1976) that the lower level of verbal intelligence by the bilingual subjects in the earlier studies (Darcy, 1953) 'may be a reflection of the fact that they are likely to have had less than native-like competence in both their languages' (Cummins, 1976: 36). Cummins (1976: 37) hypothesizes that 'the level of linguistic competence may mediate the effects of his bilingual learning experience on cognitive growth'.

In other words, the bilingual's level of competence in L1 and L2 is posited:

> as an intervening variable in the causal chain between cognitive development and more fundamental social, attitudinal, educational and cognitive factors. Specifically, there may be a threshold level of linguistic competence which a bilingual child must attain both in order to avoid cognitive deficits and allow the potentially beneficial aspects of becoming bilingual to affect his cognitive functioning. Bilingualism and unilingualism can both be thought of as instruments which individuals use to operate upon their environments. Because of its greater complexity, the bilingual instrument is more difficult to master, but once mastered has greater potential than the unilingual instrument for promoting cognitive growth. (Cummins, 1976: 37)

This direction of research looks exceedingly promising and may eventually account for a number of contradictory research findings.

To sum up, although the US and Canadian research studies frequently identify the same variables from the range of phenomena within bilingual education and see them in similar relationships, these studies illustrate the point that underlying assumptions (and bias of the researcher although I have not discussed that issue) so strongly influence the research design, the questions, and the findings that one cannot at this stage of the research extrapolate from the results of one set of studies to the other.

Although I don't deny that we need case studies, I have my reservations. I do agree with Merrill Swain (1976a: 1) on the value of psychometric evaluation research which looks at the bilingual education programs as the independent variable:

> It can provide essential feedback to the programs themselves often· resulting in program change. Furthermore, such evaluations have provided individuals considering the implementation of a bilingual program with information about the results of a variety of options, one of which may be applicable to their community given their own particular needs and characteristics. And finally, although a single evaluation carries little generalizability in and out of itself, 'such case studies are necessary if we are to begin to develop a theory of bilingual education which will enable us to generalize the evidence from the individual studies and to account for their often contradictory findings'. (C. B. Paulston, 1975b: 5) (Swain, 1976a: 1)

My reservations as far as all these studies go is very simple and probably fairly characteristic of the conflict orientation:

> . . . unless we try in some way to account for the socio-historical, cultural, and economic-political factors which lead to certain forms of bilingual education, we will never understand the consequences of that education. In other words, we need research which looks at bilingual education as the intervening[7] or dependent variable, and we don't have it.

> It is simply that medium of instruction in school programs is an intervening variable rather than the causal variable as it is always treated in all these studies on reading achievement by children from ethnic groups and languages in contact. By merely examining intervening variables, with no (or little) attempt to identify independent variables, one cannot hope to achieve any similarity and consensus in the research findings, as indeed we don't have. (C. B. Paulston, 1975b: 370, 373)

> However interesting I find the evaluation research on the bilingual education programs, I find — and that is my particular bias — that there are other questions that I consider more important.

Systems theory

> Bushnell & Rappaport's (1971) work, *Planned Change in Education: A Systems Approach,* offers an illustrative summary of assumptions and 'constructive alternatives' underlying the claims of systems theory to hold promise for a 'more rapid adaptation of our public schools to the demands of a modern society.'

From the systems perspective, the need for reform arises with evidence of system 'malfunctioning.' Using the example of a stockmarket broker, Bushnell & Rappaport present an 'information flow model' to provide the structure or network of communication flow between all participants in the school system from students to taxpayers. (R. G. Paulston, 1976: 16) (See Figure 4.1.)

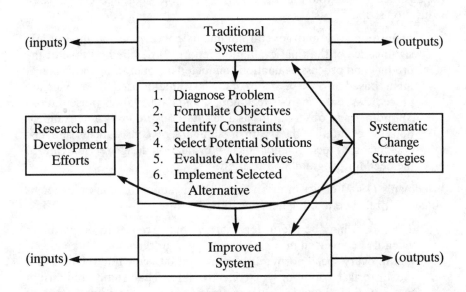

FIGURE 4.1 *A research and development strategy for planned educational change*

The problem of educational change from this perspective is essentially one of 'rationalizing existing education systems through the introduction of innovations that respond both to new social needs and to the need for greater efficiency in ongoing functions' (R. G. Paulston, 1976: 17), an apt definition of bilingual education from the viewpoint I have so far discussed it. The difficulty with the systems approach is that it sacrifices reality to 'scientific rigor.' There is rarely any attempt to identify and operationalize contextual variables like power relationships, ethnic culture conflicts, disagreements over values and the like, 'which might question the conservative notions of equilibrium and consensus inherent in the functionalist-cum-systems perspective' (R. G. Paulston, 1976: 20).

The literature on bilingual education from a systems perspective is remarkably sparse. Tucker (1976) may occasionally sound like a system analyst in his 'Summary: Research conference on immersion education for the majority child' but that is probably just a reflection of the primarily S/F approach to immersion research in Canada. An ERIC search turned up one single hit, Prochnow's (1973) 'Final evaluation accomplishment audit of the Harlandale independent school district's bilingual education program'. In the abstract, we are told that the report follows the suggested US Office of Education scope:

> 1) Introductory and general comments concerning the quality and significance of the final evaluation report; 2) detailed critique of the product and process evaluation conducted for operation and management, based on an assessment of the instruments used, data collection procedures, data analysis techniques, and data analysis presentation; 3) findings and observations as a result of on-site visits and examinations of evaluative data with a summary of consistencies and discrepancies; 4) recommendations for evaluation design revision; and 5) the need for program modification.

Friedman's (1963) criticism of an equilibrium model in economics seems equally appropriate to bilingual education:

> The model may be useful for analysis, but it ceases to be pertinent when it is converted into a normative rule for planning. To be meaningful, every social norm must be brought into concrete relation with the historical conditions of collective life. That static equilibrium mode, valid only within a parameter of carefully stated and artificial assumptions, is wholly inappropriate by this standard. (Friedman, 1963: 72)

Systems theory has not in the past been a viable approach in research in bilingual education. This section could easily have been omitted except that I wanted to point out the shortcomings of this approach so that also in the future it remain not salient in our concerns.

'Distressed liberal' genre

R. G. Paulston (1976: 24) closes the section on the equilibrium paradigm with a discussion of what he terms 'the largely atheoretical "distressed liberal" genre which, while essentially S/F in world view, calls for basic educational reform as a strategy for meliorative social reform'. This type of work avoids a discussion of the role of power and conflict, sees inequities and inefficiencies of the schools as the result of bureaucratic, teacher or parent mindlessness or ignorance but not as a consequence of social-class self-interest leading to structured inequality.

> US government agencies, foundations, and financial institutions, intervening both at home and abroad in the interests of poor people, continue to share the basic assumption of this genre, i.e. that educational reform will eventually lead in some enlightened, relatively confict-free way to more equitable, democratic social relations and conditions. (R. G. Paulston, 1976: 24)

The writings on bilingual education are amply represented in this category and we have all probably at one time or another fallen into this camp. I have discussed in 'On the moral dilemma of the sociolinguist' (C. B. Paulston, 1971), some of the concerns which can lead a linguist into this sort of a position. Because of the basically atheoretical nature of this genre of writing, I think we should recognize that it tends to weaken the research base and to trivialize scholarly support of bilingual education.

The equilibrium paradigm: conclusion

Bilingual education in the United States is necessarily closely tied to concerns of ethnic groups. We have lately experienced a resurgence of ethnic awareness which brings into question the goal of complete assimilation for these ethnic groups. Elazar & Friedman (1976) discuss this new development of ethnic affirmation in their perceptive *Moving Up: Ethnic Succession in America*. They point out that ethnic identity has often been seen as a problem that must somehow be overcome. Social scientists have often considered religious and ethnic groups as 'vestiges of a primitive past that are destined to disappear' (Elazar & Friedman, 1976: 4), but recent 'writers on the "new pluralism" have argued that racial, religious, and ethnic groups *are* a basic component of our social structure' (p. 5) who affect our institutions and are at times more powerful than economic forces in their influence.

What Elazar & Friedman are discussing in their study of ethnic groups, is in fact a paradigm shift from equilibrium theory to a conflict perspective and some recent work on bilingual education reflects that shift. As the S/F framework Larkin (1970) discusses would predict, there is considerable tension accompanying the implementation of bilingual education. However, equilibrium theory is not designed to deal with such conflict.

> With its limited ability to include, let alone explain, conflict in the calculus of change efforts, the equilibrium paradigm must now seriously compete with alternative views of social and educational reform that

see change and instability as constant and unavoidable characteristics of all social organisms and relations. (R. G. Paulston, 1976: 24)

The Conflict Paradigm

Studies of socio-economic, cultural, and educational change using variants of conflict theory have increased significantly during the past decade or so (Coser, 1956; Dahrendorf, 1959; Zeitlin, 1968; Allardt, 1971; Carnoy, 1974; Collins, 1971; Smelser, 1971; Boudon, 1974; Dreir, 1975). This work may be divided into three types of conflict 'theory' — i.e., (1) Marxist and group conflict explanations of socio-economic conflict, (2) cultural revival or revitalization explanations of value conflict, and (3) the somewhat mixed bag of anarchist and anarchist-utopian explanations of institutional conflict and constraints on human development. (R. G. Paulston, 1976: 26)

Group conflict theory

. . . all variants of conflict theory reject the evolutionists' and functionists' image of society as a system of benign self-regulating mechanisms where maintenance of social equilibrium and harmony is 'functional' and disruption of harmony is 'dysfunctional' . . . Formal education is here viewed as a part of the ideological structure which a ruling class controls to maintain its dominance over the masses, and because formal education is dependent on the dominant economic and political institutions, it cannot be a primary agent of social transformation . . . it can only follow changes in the imperatives of the economic and political social order (Gramsci, 1957; Zachariah, 1975). (R. G. Paulston, 1976: 26)

Studies of bilingual education using aspects or variants of conflict theory have increased during the last few years. The definition of the problem from a conflict perspective is no longer unequal opportunity *per se* but rather one of structured inequity, of 'persistence of poverty, intractability of inequality of incomes and inequality of economic and social opportunity' (Bowles, Gintis & Meyer, 1975–6: 263). Unequal opportunity, the existence of which is most certainly not denied, tends to be seen as a result of a condition of inequity rather than as a cause of school failure.

Consequently in conflict-oriented studies the solutions to the educational problems of bilingual programs are rarely sought in terms of technocratic efficiency; in fact, they are rarely sought within the programs themselves but rather are seen to lie outside the programs. It is in this context that we need to interpret the significance of Fishman's (1976) discussion of 'social dimensions': 'very few [empirical studies] have focused upon particular social parameters and explored their relevance to bilingual education across schools and/or across communities' (Fishman, 1976: 22b). One reason that this is so is that the majority of research on bilingual education has followed the S/F approach, and if one assumes that improved efficiency of school programs will solve problems of scholastic achievement, then one looks to instruction rather than to social factors for elucidation. On the other hand, if one assumes that formal education cannot cope with the consequences of social injustice or social inequity of which bilingual education in this country is one consequence, then Fishman's statement 'that societal factors are not merely "interesting" or "enlightening" for an understanding of bilingual education but that they represent powerful forces governing the success and failure of such programs' (Fishman, 1976: 25) points the major direction for research on bilingual education.

In this connection, a comment on Fishman's discussion of typologies of bilingual education is in order. Basically the typologies fall into two categories: (1) those which are 'school oriented' and classify by program and program outcomes (Spolsky, 1974a; Fishman & Lovas, 1970; Fishman, 1976), and (2) those which are 'context' oriented and classify by the social factors which contribute to the establishment of bilingual programs (Gaarder, n.d.; Schermerhorn, 1970; C. B. Paulston, 1975b; Spolsky, 1974b belongs here too although not discussed by Fishman); Mackey (1970) combines the two.

From a conflict perspective, it is the social factors which are seen to influence the success or failure of bilingual education programs, and hence it is clearly the derivation of 'context' oriented typologies which hold the higher priority since they are more likely to help facilitate the identification of salient social dimensions. Also, when revised and improved, 'context' oriented typologies can be seen then to function at a higher level in the ladder of theoretical abstraction (Pelto, 1970) than do school oriented typologies, and this higher level of abstraction accounts for the key weakness of the former: the difficulty in operationalizing key concepts.

The long-range goals of the programs, seen from a conflict perspective, follow the definition of the problem: to maximize equity in the distribution of wealth, goods and services; hence the emphasis is no longer on efficiency but on *equity*. This necessarily leads to disagreement over the evaluation of bilingual education programs. In the following discussion of such evaluations, I make no attempt at impartiality between the two paradigms; the discussion is clearly written from a conflict perspective and illustrative of the concerns, in this approach, with equity rather than efficiency.

Like Tucker (who had complained about a lack of consensus over the goals of bilingual education), the National Institute of Education (1975: 8) report stresses the need for aims and objectives to be 'clarified and made explicit so that progress toward the goal can be evaluated'. I don't share their concern. It is a functionalist technician's mistake to want consensual goals in order to assess the efficacy of bilingual education programs. The parents want access to goods and services for children with the least degree of damage to their sense of self, and they will vary in their interpretation of the best means to achieve that goal.

It makes a lot more sense than to use standardized tests on school achievement to assess the bilingual education programs in the United States in terms of employment figures upon leaving school, figures on drug addiction and alcoholism, suicide rates and personality disorders, i.e. indicators which measure the social pathology which accompanies social injustice rather than in terms of language skills. Many of us see the bilingual education programs as an attempt to cope with such social injustice rather than as an attempt at efficient language teaching — although the programs are that too. One of the best indicators with which to evaluate bilingual education programs are the drop-out rates. The drop-out rate for American Indians in Chicago public schools is 95%; in the bilingual-bicultural Little Big Horn High School in Chicago the drop-out rate in 1976 was 11% (*New York Times,* 1976a: 49), and I find that figure a much more meaningful indicator for evaluation of the bilingual program than any psychometric assessment of students' language skills (C. B. Paulston, 1976b).

The major assumption which underlies most work written within the conflict paradigm is that bilingual education programs can only be understood in terms of the relationship between the various interest groups and that relationship is seen as basically one of a power conflict:

> The probability is overwhelming that when two groups with different cultural histories establish contacts that are regular rather than occasional or intermittent, one of the two groups will typically assume dominance over the other. (Schermerhorn, 1970: 68)

Lenski's (1966: 17) metaphor is suggestive of the difference in world view between the two paradigms: 'where functionalists see human societies as social systems, conflict theorists see them as stages on which struggles for power and privilege take place.' This viewpoint is most clearly seen in the militant/utopian writings on bilingualism and bilingual education, as in this editorial from *Defensa:*

> En otras palabras, los *québécois* se han dado cuenta por fin de que si no ponen un ¡ hasta acá! acabarán siendo ciudadanos de tercera clase en su proprio país.
>
> Dicho de otra modo, el bilinguismo collectivo, impuesta por la dura necesidad de comer, es como una herida que no se cierra, y sangra y no deja de sangrar.
>
> Ya lo hemos dicho en otra ocasion: el dinero habla mas fuerte que la sintaxis. (*Defensa*, 1976: 3)[8]

Clearly, the research designs on bilingual education from this perspective are not likely to consider *instruction* as the independent variable nor to consider issues of language as the most salient aspects of bilingual education. There is as yet no generally accepted framework of research on bilingual education from a group conflict perspective, but Schermerhorn (1970) and my own paper, drawing on Schermerhorn (1975b), are increasingly being cited in the literature on bilingualism and bilingual education (Churchill, 1976; Cummins, 1976; Greenfield, 1976; Skutnabb-Kangas, 1976; Skutnabb-Kangas & Toukomaa, 1976). Since Schermerhorn is the most carefully considered design for research on ethnic relations, I would like to briefly review it here, focusing on the designation of variables and their relationship.

To Schermerhorn, the central question in comparative research in ethnic relations is 'what are the conditions that foster or prevent the integration of ethnic groups into their environing societies?' By *integration,* he does not necessarily mean assimilation but rather an 'active and coordinated compliance with the ongoing activities and objectives of the dominant group in that society' (Schermerhorn, 1970: 14); integration can include either assimilation/incorporation on the one hand or cultural pluralism on the other as long as the dominant and subordinate groups agree on the collective goals for the latter.

Schermerhorn sees three major causal factors in determining the nature of the relationship between ethnic groups and the process of integration. He posits as independent variables (1) the origin of the contact situation between 'the subordinate ethnics and dominant groups, such as annexation, migration, and colonization', (2) 'the degree of enclosure (institutional separation or segmentation) of the subordinate group or groups from the society-wide network of institutions and associations', and (3) 'the degree of control exercised by dominant groups over access to scarce resources by subordinate groups in a given society' (Schermerhorn, 1970: 15).

Intervening or contextual variables which will modify the effects of the independent variables are: (1) whether the dominant and subordinate groups agree on the goals for the latter, (2) whether the groups share common cultural and structural features, and (3) forms of institutional dominance, i.e. polity dominating economy or vice versa. 'The dependent variables to be explained are the interweaving patterns of integration and conflict'; the first two deal with the relationship between groups and are correlative, the third operationalizes this relation: (1) 'differential participation rates of subordinates in institutional and associated life (including rates of vertical mobility) as compared with rates for the dominant groups'; this is clearly the variable under which the institution of formal schooling and bilingual education programs are subsumed; (2) 'the extent of satisfaction or dissatisfaction of both subordinate and dominant group members with the differential patterns of participation as they see them, together with accompanying ideologies and cultural values'; this is the variable which subsumes the attitudes and reactions of all those involved in bilingual education: students, parents, community leaders, administrators, government officials, linguists and other researchers, etc. The discussions and controversy about transitional or maintenance bilingual programs would fall under this variable where the type of program is seen as a *consequence* of the other factors just outlined, not as a factor *determining* program outcomes; and (3) 'overt or covert behavior patterns of subordinates and dominants indicative of conflict and/or harmonious relations; assessment in terms of continued integration' (Schermerhorn, 1970: 15–16).

How these concepts are to be operationalized is far from clear, and the major contribution of Schermerhorn's framework to research in bilingual education is to indicate the direction of research, to make clear the futility of continued research which ignores the social and historical factors which lead to the establishment of bilingual education. At this time, the majority of work within the conflict paradigm considers bilingual education programs as the dependent variable; presumably we need to work out a framework which will allow us to consider bilingual education as an intervening variable so the dependent variables to be explained can become both scholastic achievement and social integration. It remains to be demonstrated that there is no relationship between the latter two variables in bilingual education; there well may be.

Integration, i.e. assimilation or cultural pluralism, as a dependent variable can be operationalized in terms of language maintenance and language shift. An early work on Title VII bilingual education programs, written from a group conflict perspective, was Kjolseth's seminal 'Bilingual education programs in the United States: for assimilation or pluralism?' which considered 'the *social* consequences of particular bilingual education strategies upon the changing patterns of *community* language *use*' (Kjolseth, 1972: 116). Kjolseth echoes Gaarder's concern that the bilingual programs (because they are more efficient for a number of reasons in teaching the children English) may be a one way bridge to English and complete language shift although he looks favorably on bilingualism and cultural pluralism in contrast to Gaarder. The cure for group bilingualism, from Gaarder's (1975) view, is not to learn the dominant language, not to learn English. It is an extreme and utopian position, but nevertheless it is against this background of bilingual education and language shift that the controversy regarding transitional versus maintenance programs is best interpreted.

At a conference, as reported in *Wassaja: A National Newspaper of Indian America* (1977: 15) one participant raised the issues of whether Title VII programs should

> provide a transitional bilingual program model or a maintenance bilingual program.
>
> The maintenance program provides assistance to students, with an underlying premise that a child's native language and culture is a resource that needs to be capitalized upon so as to provide the maximum opportunity for students to develop their full potential, said Morris.
>
> Finally, Morris criticized the Title VII program, saying its regulations call for 'transitional bilingual program models which function on the premise of remedial programs for bilingual, non-and-limited English speaking students alone'.

The proponents of maintenance programs favor cultural pluralism and ethnic diversity and tend to see the world in terms of conflict and competition between interest groups. Recent development has seen mobilization along ethnic boundaries as one strategy in competition for rewards (Elazar & Friedman, 1976), and maintenance of the ethnic language becomes a very visible aspect of such mobilization. Language shift remains a phenomenon which is poorly understood (Fishman, 1976; Lieberson *et al.*, 1975), and the relationship between bilingual education and language maintenance and shift is no better understood today than when Kjolseth (1972: 117) pointed out 'that there is not a single study planned to determine program effects upon community diglossia'. Fishman (1976: 21) is right in pointing out the seriousness of Gaarder's argument about the consequences of bilingual education for marked populations; we especially need to investigate the social factors which influence bilingual programs in contributing to language maintenance and shift. As a matter of fact, we don't even know whether bilingual education influences language maintenance or shift in any significant way.

An important question in studies written from a conflict perspective is *cui bono?*, 'who stands to gain?' (Gramsci, 1957), where 'gain' can be operationalized as an indicator of which group benefits in the power struggle. The literature on bilingual education is noticeable for the almost complete absence of such questions. The pious assumption is of course that the children are the ones who stand to gain, with indicators like standardized tests scores on school achievement and self-concept. I have discussed other indicators like suicide rates and school attendance figures.

Other obvious indicators are budget allocations and salary schedules. The only studies I know which consider the issue of salaries in bilingual education are Spolsky's (1974b: 57): '[the economic] impact on a local poor community cannot be underestimated.'

> In the Navajo situation, the most important outcome of bilingual education is probably related to changes in the economic and political situation. At the moment, the 53,000 Navajo students in school, 90% of whom speak Navajo, are taught by 2600 teachers, only 100 of whom speak Navajo. A decision to establish bilingual education, even a transitional variety for the first three grades, sets up a need for a thousand Navajo speaking teachers. Whatever effects this may have on the educational or linguistic situation, it is clear that it immediately provides jobs within the community for a sizeable group of people. A thousand well-paying jobs on the reservation for Navajos would lead to a greater income not just for the teachers themselves but for the community as a whole and would immediately establish within the community a well-paid middle class whose potential influence on political development of the Navajo Nation is obvious. Whatever may then be the expressed goals of a bilingual education program, it is probable that its major effect will be in this area. (Spolsky, 1974a: 23–4)

It is against this background that the controversy and discussions about ESL programs versus BE programs is best understood, and the attempts to carry out those discussions at a programmatic level of language teaching methodology only confuses the basic issue which is one of competition for scarce jobs:

The threat of bilingual education is thus a direct economic one to the present teachers and administrators. However much they may sympathize with a bilingual education program, and however much they may agree on an intellectual level with its logic and its goals, they cannot for long remain unaware that their own jobs are at stake. In these circumstances, it is not surprising that bilingual programs often face opposition from teachers and administrators. (Spolsky, 1974b: 54)

Hill-Burnett's comment that the key to access to a position lies with 'the answer to the question of who has the authority to judge whether the performance meets the standards' then becomes of crucial interest since it is a given that all groups are self-seeking and define 'performance' in terms of furthering their own interests. The controversial 'Lau Remedies' document is a case in point. There is no research on 'who has the authority' in bilingual education, on the ideology and ethnic identification[9] of administrators who control access to positions. It would seem that *who* holds control over such 'authority' will have important implications in the definitions of goals, implementations of programs, and evaluation of outcomes, yet it is a question we have not asked. It is true that ethnic groups tend to see the necessity of community control over programs as axiomatic:

We call upon city, state, and Federal institutions . . . to insure that these programs are controlled by and responsive to the needs of Latino residents. (Sevilla-Casas *et al.*, 1973)

These [Cultural Education] Centres must be Indian controlled and operated, in view of the fact that they are established for Indian purposes and use. (National Indian Brotherhood, 1972: 17)

Nevertheless, it is an issue which remains uninvestigated in formal research and one which is probably of extreme importance in explaining and predicting phenomena in bilingual education.

Whoever else gains from bilingual education, the children certainly do too, and the clearest evidence we have in the form of empirical research on language skills comes from the data on children from the Finnish working-class migrant population in Sweden. There is no research here which parallels these studies, and to my mind such research is urgent as findings of this nature constitute compelling arguments for bilingual education to S/F and conflict theorists alike. The Scandinavian data are particularly significant in that both countries are highly developed industrialized modern societies with school achievement norms both for children in Sweden and Finland. In addition, Sweden is a quasi-socialist society where problems of health-care, diet, and unemployment are not intervening variables. Such conditions are often cited as contributory factors in the lack of school achievement by minority children.

In a UNESCO report, Skutnabb-Kangas & Toukomaa (1976: 48) report on a study in which 687 Finnish students in Swedish schools, divided among 171 classes, were tested.

> The purpose of the study was to determine the linguistic level and development in both their mother tongue and Swedish of Finnish migrant children attending Swedish comprehensive school. Above all, attention was paid to the interdependence between skills in the mother tongue and Swedish, i.e. the hypothesis was tested that those who have best preserved their mother tongue are also best in Swedish. Partly related to this question the significance of the age of which the child moved to Sweden was also determined. Do those who received a firm grounding in their mother tongue by attending school in Finland have a better chance of learning Swedish than those who moved to Sweden as pre-schoolers?
>
> A second important problem is the achievement of Finnish pupils in Swedish language schools. How do Finnish migrant pupils do in theoretical and what might be called practical subjects? Does one's skill in the mother tongue have any effect on the grade given in a Swedish-language school or on other school achievement? (Skutnabb-Kangas & Toukomaa, 1976: 48)

On all non-verbal ability factors the migrant children tested out at normal or slightly above normal level, i.e. they consistently test out at a normal level of intelligence; between verbal and non-verbal factors, however, there is an 'enormous gap'. During the first 4–5 years of school 'the Finnish migrant pupils . . . remained at a level which in Finland had fewer than 10% of the poorest pupils judged in verbal tests'. In other words, their Finnish is poor (Skutnabb-Kangas & Toukomaa, 1976: 53) and so is their Swedish where 'the average level Finnish pupil had a test point score in Swedish on a level at which about 10% of the poorest Swedish pupils were placed' (p. 54).

The language development data are supported by findings from a study by Särkelä & Kuusinen (1975) who tested 182 subjects in Sweden with a rural control group in Finland. The migrant children were slightly more above average as measured by the non-verbal Raven intelligence test.

> On the other hand, the psycholinguistic ages determined by the ITPA (Illinois Test of Psycholinguistic Abilities) show that in their command of the Finnish language the pupils in Finnish-language classes in Sweden were on average 2.5–3 years behind the normal Finnish level

and the Finnish pupils in Swedish-language classes were 3–4 years behind the normal Finnish level. (Skutnabb-Kangas & Toukomaa, 1976: 55)

In general Skutnabb-Kangas & Toukomaa found that the children's rate of improvement in Swedish was not as fast as the regression in the mother tongue. Although ability factors influenced the learning of Swedish, it is very clear 'that the better a pupil has preserved his mother tongue, the better are his prerequisites for learning the second language' (Skutnabb-Kangas & Toukomaa, 1976: 78). Overwhelmingly the better a student knew Finnish (as a function of having attended school for several years in Finland), the better he learned Swedish. An examination of language skills of siblings found that those who moved from Finland at an average age of ten have preserved an almost normal Finnish language level and they also approach the normal level in Swedish of Swedish pupils. Those who moved at the age of twelve also achieve language skills comparable to those of the Swedes although learning the language takes place more slowly. The children who moved under the age of six or who were born in Sweden do not do as well. Their Swedish language development 'often stops at the age of about twelve, evidently because of their poor grounding in the mother tongue' (p. 75). Worst off are the pupils who were 7–8 when they moved to Sweden. 'The verbal development of these children, who moved just after school was beginning (children begin school at seven in Sweden) underwent serious disturbance after the move. This also has a detrimental effect on learning Swedish' (p. 75).

In an examination of the school achievement of the Finnish students, it was found that they did relatively well in mathematics, in the upper level almost as well as their Swedish classmates. But more interestingly,

The Finnish-language skills shown by the test results are fairly closely connected with the grade in mathematics. In the upper level, Finnish seems to be even more important for achievement in mathematics than Swedish — in spite of the fact that mathematics, too, is taught in Swedish. This result supports the concept that the abstraction level of the mother tongue is important for mastering the conceptual operations connected with mathematics . . . Subjects such as biology, chemistry and physics also require conceptual thinking, and in these subjects migrant children with a good mastery of their mother tongue succeeded significantly better than those who knew their mother tongue poorly. (Skutnabb-Kangas & Toukomaa, 1976: 69)

The Canadian data from Manitoba on French-speaking children also support the Finnish data. In a report entitled 'Academic achievement and language of instruction among Franco-Manitoban pupils', Hebert *et al.* (1976) also found that the pupils who did better in French, their mother tongue, also did better in English and in other academic courses. Intelligence, socio-economic level and motivation were controlled for in this study, so they could not be factors which influenced the findings. The evidence for the importance of mother tongue development seems clear, and one would wish for similar research in the United States. Basically structural-functionalist in research design, the Finnish studies nevertheless are motivated by the same concerns which are typical of a group conflict orientation. Skutnabb-Kangas's argument, based on her data, that it is highly functional within a capitalist system to withhold bilingual education from children who need it is clearly written from a conflict perspective:

> In this way the educational system contributes to ensure the perpetuation of a class society. Educational systems in Western industrial countries function as factors which preserve the social structure of society. As the educational system functions in the interests of the majority, and as the majority even in the future will need workers at the assembly lines, the educational system reproduces the immigrants' work and social structure, even when the system's official objective is to give the migrant children the same possibilities which the children in the receiver (host) country have. From this point of view one can understand the function of the migrant children's semilingualism as a factor which transfers and increases social inequality. (Skutnabb-Kangas, 1976: 35, my translation)

The Finnish UNESCO report is interesting, then, in that its authors are able to combine the ideology and concerns of group conflict theorists with a research design typical of S/F research. It is in fact one of the few attempts we have of a dialectical orientation in research of bilingual education.

Cultural revival and social movement theory

The literature on culture change and culture conflict applied to educational change is exceedingly sparse. It may be recalled that functional theory assumes a high degree of normative consensus across social systems, while conflict theory posits normative consensus or an ethos shared across major social groups, i.e., the working class, the middle class, and conflict between classes. Cultural revitalization-theory, in contrast, focuses not on social classes but, according to Wallace (1956), on 'deliberate organized conscious efforts by members of a society to construct a more satisfying culture'. Such efforts are viewed as constantly recurring phenomena, a type of culture-creating activity in collective efforts of varying size which seeks social and cultural change that may take place at local or national levels. (R. G. Paulston, 1976: 30)

Culture change

The literature on culture change applied to bilingual education is also very sparse, and we do not know what effect bilingual education may have on the culture of ethnic groups. One obvious resource of ethnic groups, which can be used in stressing ethnic awareness and identity of the members, is the mother tongue. With the recent trend toward ethnic mobilization, we see both language maintenance programs and language revival programs in which the mother tongue serves to reinforce the ethnic boundaries of the group (Barth, 1969; Spolsky, 1974b).

The most extreme form of ethnic mobilization occurs in what Wallace (1956: 265) has termed revitalization movements, 'deliberate, organized, conscious efforts by members of a society to construct a more satisfying culture'. For Wallace, this process involves a cultural transformation of the group. For the purposes of this paper, I will extend the term to include ethnic revival movements as well (which may not be involved in a cultural transformation) since Wallace's (1975: 22–3) concept of 'revolutionary phase' applies to both movements.

In his 'Schools in revolutionary and conservative societies', Wallace (1975) discusses the learning priorities of the two types of society:

What a man is expected to do in his life will, in part, depend on whether he lives in a revolutionary, conservative, or reactionary society. And what he is expected to do determines what he is expected to learn. (Wallace, 1975: 21).

He outlines a model of learning priorities as shown in Figure 4.2.

Wallace assigns very specific meanings to the terms *technic, morality* and *intellect.* By technic he refers to learning as a process of 'reliability increase of action' through stimulus, reinforcement and motivation; technic is learning 'how to'. Morality, on the other hand, stresses 'what'. Morality concerns one particular kind of socially approved value:

This kind of value is the conception that one's own behaviour, as well as the behaviour of others, should not merely take into consideration the attitude of the community, but should actively advance, or at least nor retard, its welfare. (Wallace, 1975: 18)

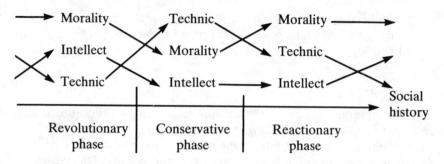

Source: Wallace (1975: 26)

FIGURE 4.2   *Learning priorities in revolutionary, conservative, and reactionary societies*

Although most commonly practiced in the humble endurance of discomfort by inconspicuous people, it is 'most conspicuously exemplified by such heroic actions as the soldier's throwing himself on a handgrenade in order to smother the blast and save his buddies' (Wallace, 1975: 18). The criterion for morality is its potential for sacrifice, and all ethnic groups in the revolutionary phase have sacrificial heroes as leaders, i.e. leaders who are willing to risk freedom or life for the cause; Cesar Chavez and La Causa is a good example.

Groups undergoing a revolutionary phase will always stress moral learning, and conflicts are certain to arise when a revitalization movement takes place within a conservative society where technic has the highest learning priority, i.e. 'in conservative societies, schools prepare people not for sacrifice but for jobs' (R. G. Paulston, 1972: 478). Language skills in the official language must be seen as an aspect of technic, an aspect of preparation for jobs. The mother tongue, on the other hand, is an aspect of moral learning, reaffirming the solidarity and cultural uniqueness of the ethnic group, underscoring the need to teach the moral values of good and evil, right and wrong, the values of the old gods, in the language in which those values were originally transmitted. Reaffirmation of cultural values is frequently a part of the moral teaching, especially among ethnic groups who prior to the revitalization movement have been taught by the dominant group to have nothing but contempt for their own culture.

The conflict over learning priorities explains the extreme importance of control over local educational institutions, without which the ethnic group will not be able to implement its priorities. I have frequently heard commented among my colleagues that the best bilingual schools are those that are under community control — be it Navajo or Chicano. I am not certain what 'best' means in this connection. In my (C. B. Paulston, 1975a: 25) discussion of the Erickson *et al.* (1969) report in an earlier paper, I pointed out that 'rhetoric about cultural pluralism accounts for little if the objectives are not implemented'; the community run Navajo school, as measured by the achievement test batteries from the California Test Bureau, was markedly inferior to the government run school academically. I was at the time interested in investigating only the learning of English language skills, but even so that statement — and the evaluation itself — shows our typical tendency to assess and evaluate the schooling of groups undergoing a revitalization movement with moral learning as the priority in terms of the standards of the conservative society — the standards of technique.

The function of bilingual education in ethnic revival movements is obviously an important one, but one we know very little about. A group conflict perspective is not helpful in trying to account for culture-change as this theory focuses on conflict *between* the various groups. Wallace's framework allows us to focus on change within the group as it becomes 'revitalized,' but we need to explore the role of language within such revitalization movements, especially the function of language in the mechanism of ethnic boundary maintenance.

Culture conflict

The literature on culture conflict applied to bilingual education at the national level is also exceedingly sparse, but a number of studies exist at the programmatic level. These studies of culture conflict differ from group conflict studies in that the latter tend to focus on conflict which is caused by structured inequality, i.e. they focus on aspects of social structure, of major institutional activities of society, like economic and political life. The studies on culture conflict, on the other hand, tend to be ethnographic in nature and focus on conflict which is caused by an incomplete knowledge and understanding of the other group's culture as its norms and values are expressed in overt behavior.

Hymes (1970) sketches in 'Bilingual education: linguistic vs. sociolinguistic bases' a general theoretical framework for such research. Culture conflict in communication is interpreted as 'interference not only between phonologies and grammars, but also between norms of interaction and interpretation of speech' (Hymes 1970: 74):

The notion 'ways of speaking' calls particular attention to the fact that members of a speech community have a knowledge such that speech is interpretable as pertaining to one or another genre, and as instancing one or another speech act and event. (Hymes, 1970: 74)

Susan Philips (1970) used this framework in her work on the Warm Springs Indian Reservation in accounting for the children's school failure. The children's native ways of speaking and strategies for learning are very different from those of the Anglo school's, and consequently 'Indian children fail to participate verbally in the classroom interaction because the social conditions for participation to which they have become accustomed in the Indian community are lacking'.

> Educators cannot assume that because Indian children (or children from other cultural backgrounds than that which is implicit in American classrooms) speak English, or are taught it in school, that they have also assimilated all of the sociolinguistic rules underlying interaction in classrooms and other non-Indian social situations where English is spoken. (Philips, 1970: 95)

Culture conflict or interference in the classroom is a topic of immense importance in teacher training, and much of this literature is directed at the teacher (Aarons *et al.,* 1969; Abrahams & Troike, 1972; Burger, 1971; Cazden *et al.,* 1972; C. B. Paulston, 1974; Spolsky, 1972; Turner, 1973). The assumption which underlies these studies is that once the teacher understands that the children function with other sociolinguistic rules, with other rules of communicative competence, he will adjust his ways and culture interference in the classroom will be minimized. Philips is unusual in this regard:

> The teachers who make these adjustments, and not all do, are sensitive to the inclinations of their students and want to teach them through means to which they most readily adapt. However, by doing so, they are avoiding teaching the Indian children how to communicate in precisely those contexts in which they are least able, and most need to learn how to communicate if they are to do well in school. (Philips, 1970: 88)

She ends her paper by saying that the children must be taught 'the rules for appropriate speech usage', i.e. that they must be taught the ways of speaking, acceptable to the dominant culture. This is a troublesome matter and an issue about which we know virtually nothing. In spite of all the rhetoric about bilingual-bicultural education I don't know of any research on the Title VII programs which deals with the issue of bicultural teaching. To the degree that the bicultural component of Title VII programs is discussed, this discussion invariably deals with aspects of the home culture of the children, the culture whose sociolinguistic rules the children already know. I know of no work on attempts to teach the children Anglo culture, yet Philips holds such teaching crucial for the scholastic success of the children, and she may be right. The French certainly think so:

> If these children are going to live in France, it would be a bad thing and not conducive to good integration to leave them in contact with staff from their countries of origin, since these children already have a strong tendency to follow their native customs so that there is a danger of counter-adaptation. (Council of Europe, 1976: 31)

Utopian Perspectives

> Anarchistic and utopian theories of social change share the Marxian goal of radical social transformation, and the concern of cultural revival and revitalization movements for individual renewal. In marked contrast to all other previously noted theories seeking to explain and predict educational reform processes, they rarely bother to validate their call to reform with the findings and methods of social science, or to put their theory to practice (Idenberg, 1974). The utopians' often insightful critiques of existing inequalities and 'evils' in education may serve to provoke impassioned discussion (Rusk, 1971; Graubard, 1972; Marin *et al.*, 1975), but utopian analysis rarely takes into account how existing oppressive power relationships and lack of tolerance for 'deviance' or change in any given social setting will influence reform efforts of whatever scope or magnitude (Freire, 1973). Typically the utopians begin with a critical analysis of socio-educational reality and rather quickly wind up in a dream world. (R. G. Paulston, 1976: 33–4)

Because of the provocative nature of their work, we are all familiar with names like Goodman (1960) and Illich (1971), but none of these utopian theories have been used in any serious attempts to understand the phenomena of bilingual education.

However, the literature on bilingual education abounds with its own utopian statements which tend to fall into three categories: romantic/utopian, militant/utopian and visionary/utopian.

A very large share of the literature tends to romanticize what bilingual education is and can do:

A new humanism in education has very quickly brought revolutionary changes to the public school systems of the United States . . . The remarkable dispatch with which bilingual educational projects have been implemented in this country during the past year bespeaks the altruism and idealism of teachers and administrators who have activated them. For in order to institute these programs, it has been necessary for the teachers themselves to write and develop their own teaching materials, translate textbooks . . . (Byrd, 1974: 39)

'La verdad es que la mayoría de los programas bilingües andan cojeando' — 'The truth is that the majority of the bilingual programs only limp along' (Pascual, 1976: 5). Pascual's comment is based on hundreds of classroom visits, and the discrepancy between the reality of the 'salones de clase' where the children learn to read from experience charts — 'endless charts prepared by aides or teachers who guess at the orthography or rather at times invent it' (Pascual, 1976: 6, my translation) and the view of altruistic teachers in pursuit of a new humanism is not very helpful. Bilingual education is not a search for the Holy Grail, and unrealistic expectations only harm its future development.

How helpful the militant/utopian statements on bilingual education are is a question which deserves to be studied in the context of ethnic mobilization. It may be simplistic to write off such statements as *bellas palabras* and we ought to know something of the process by which voters organize along ethnic boundaries and gain control of local school boards. The following citation directed to Mayor Daley and the Chicago City Council is clearly a political document.

Our conference brought together Latinos in Chicago who have fought to establish bilingual-bicultural human service programs that are responsive to and controlled by the Latino community.

These programs were established both through battles with established institutions and by setting up alternative facilities which bypassed irrelevant institutional services. Each of these programs is staffed and controlled by Latino community residents.

These bilingual-bicultural programs are desperately fighting to stem the tide of oppression by Anglo society and institutions as seen in an 80% drop-out rate, poverty and urban renewal.

However, these programs are not enough. We call upon city, state, and Federal institutions:

(1) To allocate a fair share of its resources to bilingual-bicultural Latino programs.
(2) To insure that these programs are controlled by and responsive to the needs of Latino residents.
(3) To see to it that Anglo institutions stop pressuring Latinos to become 'Americanized' but recognize that our country can be strengthened by many different languages and cultures.
(4) To insure that institutions serving Latinos make significant changes in their programs, resources and staff so that they can more effectively serve our people.

(Sevilla-Casas *et al.*, 1973)

But we know nothing from any kind of organized research efforts about the effect of this and similar documents. Nor do we know very much about mainstream tolerance for such cultural 'deviance', but clearly the future of bilingual education in the United States is dependent upon such tolerance. An editorial in the *New York Times* (1976b) gave us a recent indication of how far one can expect such tolerance:

In a recent editorial on bilingual education, we expressed concern over a growing tendency to misuse an essentially sound pedagogical tool toward the wrong educational and political ends. Specifically, we argued that the maintenance of non-English speaking enclaves points the road to 'cultural, economic, and political devisiveness'. . . . There are clearly some who view non-English speaking enclaves as attractive bases from which to enhance their own political power. Whatever short-term political pressures might be gained from such enclaves, those who in the process are denied speedy entry into the English-speaking mainstream are saddled with persistent economic and political disadvantages . . . But none of these goals causes us to modify our position that the purpose of bilingual education must be 'to create English-speaking Americans with the least possible delay'. (*New York Times*, 1976b: A26)

Finally, it should be noted that utopian writings on bilingual education usually are atheoretical in nature and so provide us with data on the course of bilingual education rather than with the means toward further understanding. The issues raised in the Chicago document and in the *Times* editorial lend themselves best to interpretation from a group conflict perspective. What utopian writings do best is to sketch a vision and to reaffirm goodwill of decent men as in these words, written in 1912 by the President of the University of New Mexico:

I make no doubt that once the people of this State realize the importance of the [Spanish language] issue and the vast results which may
accrue from it, both for State and Nation, a movement could be set on
foot which, with representation properly made to the chief executive
and the national legislature, would secure for New Mexico a federal
appropriation sufficient to fund and endow for many years to come, a
Spanish American College for the purpose of developing and utilizing
to the utmost the inheritance of our fellow citizens in the Spanish language. While a proposal of this sort, considered as a mere act of tardy
justice to a long neglected people, might fail of effect, yet the national
advantage secured thereby would assuredly win sympathy and support
for the plan. (Gray, 1912: 6)

Conclusion

I have attempted in this paper to show that a discussion of the 'theoretical and programmatic dimensions of bilingual education' must first take
into account an analysis of the various theoretical frameworks which apply
to bilingual education. Not only the formal research design but also the
alternative assumptions, goals and strategies follow from the theoretical
perspective. An exploration, then, of the range of various theoretical perspectives on bilingual education will allow:

(1) an identification of the world view and ideological orientation which is
    inherent within each theoretical perspective. Science is not value free,
    and by being able to recognize the assumptions implicit in work charac-
    teristic of specific theoretical orientations, one can better deal with such
    values;
(2) an examination of alternative questions and an understanding of the
    theoretical implications which the selection of particular questions
    entails;
(3) and finally, which remains to be done, the development of a dialectical
    research perspective in bilingual education, which would help specify
    the theoretical approach most likely to be fruitful in answering questions
    of a specified nature.

Appendix

TABLE 4.2 *Relations between theories of social and educational change/'reform'*

Social change Paradigms	'Theories'	Illustrative linked assumptions concerning educational-change potentials and processes			
		Re preconditions for educational change	*Re rationales for educational change*	*Re scope and process of educational change*	*Re major outcomes sought*
	Evolutionary	State of evolutionary readiness	Pressure to move to an evolutionary stage	Incremental and adaptive; 'natural history' approach	New stage of institutional evolutional adaption
	Neo-evolutionary	Satisfactory completion of earlier stages	Required to support 'national modernization' efforts	'Institution building' using Western models and technical assistance	New 'higher' state of education and social differentiation/specialization
Equilibrium	Structural-functionist	Altered functional & structural requisites	Social system need provoking an educational response; exogenous threats	Incremental adjustment of existing institutions, occasionally major	Continued 'homeostasis' or 'moving' equilibrium; 'human capital' and national 'development'
	Systems	Technical expertise in 'systems management' 'Rational decision making' and 'needs assessment'	Need for greater efficiency in system's operation and goal achievement; i.e. response to a system 'malfunction'	Innovative 'problem solving' in existing systems: i.e. research and development approach	Improved 'efficiency' re cost benefits; adoption of innovations

TABLE 4.2 *Continued*

Paradigms	Social change 'Theories'	Illustrative linked assumptions concerning educational-change potentials and processes			
		Re preconditions for educational change	Re rationales for educational change	Re scope and process of educational change	Re major outcomes sought
Conflict	Marxian	Elite's awareness of need for change, or shift of power to socialist rulers and educational reformers	To adjust correspondence between social relations of production and social relations of schooling	Adjustive incremental following social mutations or radical restructuring with Marxist predominance	Formation of integrated workers, i.e. the new 'Socialist Man'
	Group conflict	Increased political power and political awareness of working class	Demands for social justice and social equality	Large-scale national reforms through 'democratic' institutions and processes	Eliminate 'educational privilege' and 'elitism'; create a more equalitarian society
	Cultural revitalization	Rise of a collective effort to revive or create 'a new culture.' Social tolerance for 'deviant' normative movements and their educational programs	Rejection of conventional schooling as forced acculturation. Education needed to support advance toward movement goals	Creation of alternative schools or educational settings. If movement captures polity, radical change in national educational ideology and structure	Inculcate new normative system. Meet movement's recruitment, training and solidarity needs
	Anarchistic utopian	Creation of supportive settings; growth of critical consciousness; social pluralism	Free man from institutional and social constraints. Enhance creativity need for 'life-long learning'	Isolated 'freeing up' of existing programs and institutions, or create new learning modes and settings, i.e. a 'learning society'	Self-renewal and participation. Local control of resources and community; elimination of exploitation and alienation

Source: R. G. Paulston, 1976: vi–vii

TABLE 4.3   *Order and conflict theories of social problems as competing ideologies*

Order perspective	Conflict perspective

1. Underlying social perspective and value positions (ideal)

(a) *Image of man and society*

Society as a natural boundary-maintaining system of action	Society as a contested struggle between groups with opposed aims and perspectives
Transcendent nature of society, and entity *sui generis,* greater than and different from the sum of its parts; lack of transcendence as lack of social control means anomy	Immanent conception of society and the social relationship; men are society; society is the extension of man, the indwelling of man; the transcendence of society is tantamount to the alienation of man from his own social nature
Positive attitude toward the maintenance of social institutions	Positive attitude toward change

(b) *Human nature*

Homo duplex, man half egoistic (self-nature), half altruistic (socialized nature), ever in need of restraints for the collective good	*Homo laborans,* existential man, the active creator of himself and society through practical and autonomous social action

or

Tabula rasa, man equated with the socialization process

or

Homo damnatus, the division into morally superior and morally inferior men

(c) *Values*

The social good: balance, stability, authority, order, quantitative growth ('moving equilibrium')	Freedom as autonomy, change, action, qualitative growth

TABLE 4.3 *Continued*

Order perspective	Conflict perspective
2. Modes of 'Scientific' analysis	
Natural-science model: quest for general and universal laws and repeated patterns gleaned through empirical research	Historical model: quest for understanding (Verstehen) through historical analysis of unique and changing events; possible use of ideal type of generalization based on historically specific patterns
Structural-functional analysis	
Multiple causality; theory characterized by high level of abstraction, but empirical studies marked by low level of generalization (separation of theory from application)	Unicausality; high or low level of theoretical generalization; union of theory and practice in social research and social action
Conditions of objectivity; accurate correspondence of concepts to facts; rigid separation of observer and facts observed — passive, receptive theory of knowledge	Utility in terms of observer's interests; objectivity discussed in the context of subjectivity-activistic theory of knowledge
Analysis begins with culture as major determinant of order and structure and proceeds to personality and social organization	Analysis begins with organization of social activities or with growth and maintenance needs of man and proceeds to culture
Dominant concepts: ahistorical; high level of generality; holistic; supra-individual concepts; ultimate referent for concepts — system needs considered universally (i.e. the functional prerequisites of any social system) or relativistically (i.e. present maintenance requirements of a particular social system)	Historical, dynamic; low level of generality and high level of historical specificity; ultimate referent for concepts — human needs considered universally (i.e. man's species nature) or relativistically (demands of particular contenders for power); referent often the future or an unrealized state of affairs

TABLE 4.3   *Continued*

Order perspective	Conflict perspective

3. Order and conflict theories of social problems and deviation

(a) *Standards for the definition of health and pathology*

Health equated with existing values of a postulated society (or a dominant group in the society), ideological definition	Health equated with unrealized standards (the aspirations of subordinate but rising groups), utopian definition

(b) *Evaluation of deviant behavior*

Pathological to the functioning of the social system	Possibly progressive to the necessary transformation of existing relationships

(c) *Explanation of deviation or a social problem*

A problem of anomy in adequate control over competing groups in the social system; disequilibrium in the existing society	A problem of self-alienation, being thwarted in the realization of individual and group goals; a problem of illegitimate social control and exploitation

(d) *Implied ameliorative action*

Extension of social control (further and more efficient institutionalization of social system values); adjustment of individuals to system needs; working within the system; the administrative solution	Rupture of social control; radical transformation of existing patterns of interaction; revolutionary change of the social system

4. Order and conflict theories as socially situated vocabularies

Dominant groups: the establishment and administrators of the establishment	Subordinate groups aspiring for greater power
Contemporary representatives: Parsonian and Mertonian approach to social problems as a liberal variant of order models; politically conservative approaches	C. W. Mills, new left (SNCC, SDS, etc.) approaches and old left (socialistic and communistic)

Source: Horton, 1966: 7

TABLE 4.4 *A process model suggested for case study analysis/evaluation of national educational-reform efforts*

Reform stages

1. Identification of arguments re: need for change in socioeconomic or cultural contexts	2. Diagnosis of implications for change in educational system and in contextual relations	3. Elaboration of 'treatment', i.e. planning alternatives in educational structures	4. Evaluation of normative, structural and behavioral changes sought, and unexpected outcomes
What values, ideology, i.e. normative premises? Who advocates? Who rejects? etc.	What social and educational change theory and biases? Whose expertise? Who attempts to discredit? etc.	How determined and justified re: 1 and 2? Who controls implementation? Who obstructs? etc.	What criteria? Whose goals? How determined? Who 'wins'? Who 'loses'? Relations to 1 and 2? etc.

Source: R. G. Paulston, 1976: 46

Acknowledgments

As is obvious from a reading of the paper, I am much indebted to the thinking and writing of Rolland G. Paulston. I have gained much from our many discussions on the topic of this paper and of his *Conflicting Theories of Social and Educational Change: A Typological Review,* and I gratefully acknowledge his influence on my own thoughts.

Notes

1. In this paper I am using the standard US Office of Education definition of bilingual education:

   Bilingual education is the use of two languages, one of which is English, as mediums of instruction for the same pupil population in a well organized program which encompasses part or all of the curriculum and includes the study of the history and culture associated with the mother tongue. A complete program develops and maintains the children's self esteem and a legitimate pride in both cultures.

2. The censure of Jensen's work by the members of the Linguistic Society of America at the annual conference business meeting in St Louis, 1971, provides us with a perfect example of a paradigm clash. The questions and the findings of Jensen's work were so unpalatable to the linguists that although only a handful of linguists present had actually read 'How can we boost IQ and scholastic achievement?', the overwhelming majority did not hesitate to condemn his work.

3. Cf. the wording of the Supreme Court's Lau versus Nichols opinion 'There is no equality of treatment merely by providing students with the same facilities, textbooks, teachers, and curriculum; for students who do not understand English are effectively foreclosed from any meaningful education' (Geffert *et al.*, 1975: 8).

4. Note the Court's insistence on the group; they are not concerned with individual failure: 'For me [Mr Justice Blackmun], numbers are at the heart of this case, and my concurrence is to be understood accordingly' (Geffert *et al.*, 1975: 10).

5. Nor do the St Lambert children really demonstrate the opposite: '. . . this difference . . . (views of French Canadians were generally more favorable amongst the experimental group than amongst English controls) did not reach reliably significant proportions' (Bruck & Swain, 1976: 491). After seven years, they can only talk about trends in desired directions. Genesee (1974) found no difference between the immersion group and the control group.

6. For the record, it should be pointed out that the perception of this dichotomy (Tucker, 1977; Greenfield, 1976) is a considerable simplification of fact. It would be more correct to say that the immersion programs do not incorporate the ESL techniques that we associate with the audio-lingual method, such as oral drills. But the early classes abound with ESL techniques from the direct method as well as from a cognitive code approach. To illustrate, in one third grade, a boy came up to me and said in perfect French: 'Madame, could you tell me if this (pointing to a word) is a verb?' His task was a controlled composition in which he had to rewrite all the present tense verbs in the imperfect. He had just gotten stung on *souvent* and wanted to make sure this time. The point is of course that controlled composition, where the teaching point is a specific grammar pattern, is an ESL technique *par excellence*.

Now it is true that French-speaking children spend much more time in school on the morphology of their language than do English-speaking children, but even so it is misleading to imply that the immersion children study language arts just as do native speaking children; they don't in the early grades.

The language teaching specialist in me cannot but wish for some systematic research on this aspect of the immersion programs. None exists, and these comments are based on class visits, discussions with teachers, administrators and researchers and a familiarity with the literature.

7. Wallace Lambert points out that I use the term 'intervening variable' differently from how it is used by psychologists, and he is right. To psychologists, 'intervening variable is a term invented to account for internal and directly unobservable psychological processes that in turn account for behavior . . . An intervening variable is an "in-the-head" variable. It cannot be seen, heard, or felt. It is inferred from behavior' (Kerlinger, 1973). Social scientists tend not to use the term (Pelto, 1970; Sjoberg & Nett, 1968) but Schermerhorn (1970: 15) does in the sense of 'contextual variables that modify the effects of independent variables' and which help account for the conditions for and the modes of integration of ethnic groups; intervening variables in this sense are perfectly observable variables, like cultural congruence. I use the term in this latter meaning.

8. 'In other words, the québécois have finally realized that if they don't say 'That's enough' they will end up as third-class citizens in their own country. Put in another way, group bilingualism, imposed by the harsh necessity to eat, is like a wound which will not close and bleeds and will not stop bleeding. As we have said before: money speaks louder than syntax.' [My translation.]

9. It needs to be pointed out that ethnic identification is not isomorphic with genetic background. Some claim or are granted honorary membership in ethnic groups, like Gaarder who is editor of *Defensa*, while others are perfectly assimilated to Anglo values in spite of their ethnic background of which only their surname bears evidence. It has been my experience that conservative schoolboards and the like tend to favor the latter as administrators in bilingual education.

References

AARONS, A. *et al*. 1969, Linguistic-cultural differences and American education. *Florida FL Reporter* 7, 1.

ABRAHAMS, R. and TROIKE, R. 1972, *Language and Culture Diversity in American Education*. Englewood Cliffs, NJ: Prentice-Hall.

ALLARDT, E. 1971, Culture, structure, and revolutionary ideologies. *International Journal of Comparative Sociology* 12 (March), 24–40.

ANDERSSON, T. and BOYER, M. 1970, *Bilingual Schooling in the United States*. Austin, Texas: Southwest Educational Development Laboratory.

APPLEGATE, R. B. 1975, The language teacher and the rules of speaking. *TESOL Quarterly* 9, 3.

BARTH, F. (ed.) 1969, *Ethnic Groups and Boundaries*. Boston: Little, Brown and Company.

BENDIX, R. and LIPSET, S. (eds) 1966, *Class, Status and Power*. New York: The Free Press.

BOUDON, R. 1974, *Education, Opportunity, and Social Inequality: Changing Prospects in Western Society*. New York: Wiley-Interscience.

BOWLES, S. and GINTIS, H. 1975, *Schooling in Capitalist America: Educational Reform and the Contradictions of Economic Life.* New York: Basic Books.
BOWLES, S., GINTIS, H. and MEYER, P. 1975–6, Education, IQ and the legitimation of the social division of labor. *Berkeley Journal of Sociology* 20, 233–64.
BRUCK, M. and SWAIN, M. 1976, Cognitive and attitudinal consequences of bilingual schooling. *International Journal of Psycholinguistics.*
BURGER, H. 1971, *Ethno-Pedagogy: Cross-Cultural Teaching Techniques.* Albuquerque, NM: Southwestern Cooperative Educational Laboratory.
BUSHNELL, D. S. and RAPPAPORT, D. (eds) 1971, *Planned Change in Education: A Systems Approach.* New York: Harcourt, Brace, Jovanovich.
BYRD, S. 1974, Bilingual education: Report on the International Bilingual-Bicultural Conference, May 1974. *ADFL-Bulletin of the Association of Departments of Foreign Languages* 6, 1.
CARNOY, M. 1974, *Education and Cultural Imperialism.* New York: David McKay.
CAZDEN, C. *et al.* 1972, *The Function of Language in the Classroom.* New York: Teachers College Press.
CHURCHILL, S. 1976, Recherches recentes sur le bilinguisme et l'education des francophones minoritaires au Canada: l'example ontarien. In M. SWAIN (ed.) *Bilingualism in Canadian Education, Yearbook,* Canadian Society for the Study of Education.
CICOUREL, A. 1970, The acquisition of social structure: towards a developmental sociology of language and meaning. In J. DOUGLAS (ed.) *Existential Society.* New York: Appleton.
COHEN, A. and SWAIN, M. 1976, Bilingual education: The 'Immersion Model' in the North American context. *TESOL Quarterly* 10, 1, 45–53.
COLLINS, R. 1971, Functional and conflict theories of educational stratification. *American Sociological Review* 36 (December), 1002–8.
COSER, L. 1956, *The Functions of Social Conflict.* New York: Free Press.
Council of Europe 1976, *Factors which Influence the Integration of Migrants' Children into Pre-School Education in France.* Council for Cultural Co-operation, Strasbourgh.
CUMMINS, J. 1976, The influence of bilingualism on cognitive growth: a synthesis of research findings and explanatory hypotheses. *Working Papers on Bilingualism* No. 9, 1–43.
DAHRENDORF, R. 1959, *Class and Class Conflict in Industrial Society.* Stanford: Stanford University Press.
DARCY, N. 1953, A review of the literature on the effects of bilingualism upon the measurement of intelligence. *Journal of Genetic Psychology* 82, 21–57.
Defensa 1970, Boletin de la Liga Nacional Defensora del Idioma Español. 4225 North 23 Street, Arlington, Virginia 22207.
DREIR, P. 1975, Power structures and power struggles. In *New Directions in Power Structure Research. The Insurgent Sociologist* 5 (Spring) (special issue), 233–7.
ELAZAR, D. and FRIEDMAN, M. 1976, *Moving Up: Ethnic Succession in America.* New York: Institute on Pluralism and Group Identity of the American Jewish Committee.
ENGLE, P. L. 1975, *The Use of Vernacular Languages in Education: Language Medium in Early School Years for Minority Language Groups.* Arlington, Va.: Center for Applied Linguistics.

ERICKSON, D. *et al.* 1969, *Community School at Rough Rock — An Evaluation for the Office of Economic Opportunity*. US Department of Commerce Springfield, Va.: Clearinghouse for Federal Scientific and Technical Information.

ERVIN-TRIPP, S. 1973, *Language Acquisition and Communicative Choice*. Stanford: Stanford University Press.

FINOCCHIARO, M. and KING, P. 1966, *Bilingual Readiness in Earliest School Years*. Washington, DC: Office of Education.

FISHMAN, J. 1976, Bilingual education: The state of social science inquiry. Manuscript. Center for Applied Linguistics.

FISHMAN, J. and LOVAS, J. 1970, Bilingual education in sociolinguistic perspectives. *TESOL Quarterly* 4, 215–22.

FREIRE, P. 1971, *Pedagogy of the Oppressed*. New York: Herder and Herder.

—— 1973, *Education for Critical Consciousness*. New York: Seabury Press.

FRIEDMAN, J. 1963, Regional economic policy for developing areas. *Regional Science Association Papers* 4, 42–65.

GAARDER, B. n.d. Political perspective on bilingual education. Manuscript.

—— 1975, Las consecuencias del bilingüismo. Manuscript.

GARFINKEL, H. 1967, *Studies in Ethnomethodology*. Englewood Cliffs, NJ: Prentice-Hall.

GEFFERT, H. *et al.* 1975. *The Current Status of US Bilingual Education Legislation*. Arlington, Va.: Center for Applied Linguistics.

GENESEE, F. *et al.* 1974, *Evaluation of the 1973–74 Pilot Grade XI French Immersion Class*. Montreal: The Protestant School Board of Greater Montreal.

GOFFMAN, E. 1959, *The Presentation of Self in Everyday Life*. New York: Doubleday.

—— 1961, *Encounters*. Indianapolis: Bobbs-Merrill.

GOODMAN, P. 1960, *Growing Up Absurd*. New York: Alfred Knopf.

GRAMSCI, A. 1957, *The Modern Prince*. London: Lawrence and Wishart.

GRAUBARD, A. 1972, *Free the Children: Radical Reform and the Free School Movement*. New York: Pantheon Books.

GRAY, E. D. McQ. 1912, The Spanish language in Mexico: A national resource. *Bulletin University of Mexico* 1, 2.

GREENFIELD, T. B. 1976, Bilingualism, multiculturalism, and the crises of purpose in Canada. In M. SWAIN (ed.) *Bilingualism in Canadian Education, Yearbook*. Canadian Society for the Study of Education.

GRIMSHAW, A. 1973, Rules, social interaction, and language behavior. *TESOL Quarterly* 7, 2, 99–115.

HEBERT, R. *et al.* 1976, Summary: Academic achievement and language instruction among Franco-Manitoban pupils. Manuscript. Report to the Manitoba Department of Education.

HERRNSTEIN, R. 1971, IQ. *Atlantic Monthly*.

HILL-BURNETT, J. 1976, Commentary: Paradoxes and dilemmas. *Anthropology and Education Quarterly* 7, 4, 37–8.

HOLMES, J. and BROWN, D. 1976, Developing sociolinguistic competence in a second language. *TESOL Quarterly* 10, 4, 423–31.

HOMANS, G. C. 1950, *The Human Group*. New York: Harcourt, Brace, and World.

HORTON, J. 1966, Order and conflict theories of social problems as competitive ideologies. *American Journal of Sociology* 71, 701–13.

HYMES, D. 1970, Bilingual education: Linguistic vs. sociolinguistic bases. In J. ALATIS (ed.) *Bilingualism and Language Contact*. 21st Annual Roundtable, Georgetown University.

—— 1972, On communicative competence. In J. B. PRIDE and J. HOLMES (eds) *Sociolinguistics*. Harmondsworth, England: Penguin Books.

IDENBERG, P. J. 1974, Education and Utopia. R. RYBA and B. HOLMES (eds) *Recurrent Education: Concepts and Policies for Lifelong Education*. London: The Comparative Education Society of Europe.

ILLICH, I. 1971, *Deschooling Society*. New York: Harper and Row.

JACOBSON, R. 1976, Incorporating sociolinguistic norms into an EFL program. *TESOL Quarterly* 10, 4, 411–22.

JACOBY, N. H. 1969, The progress of peoples: Toward a theory and policy of development with external aid. Santa Barbara: Center for the Study of Democratic Institutions.

JENSEN, A. 1969, How can we boost IQ and scholastic achievement? *Harvard Educational Review* 39, 1.

JOHN, V. and HORNER, V. 1971, *Early Childhood Bilingual Education*. New York: Modern Language Association.

KERLINGER, F. N. 1973, *Foundations of Behavioral Research*. New York: Holt, Rinehart and Winston.

KJOLSETH, R. 1972, Bilingual education programs in the United States: for assimilation or pluralism? In B. SPOLSKY *The Language Education of Minority Children*. Rowley, Mass.: Newbury House.

KUHN, T. S. 1971, *The Structure of Scientific Revolutions*. Chicago: University of Chicago Press.

LAMBERT, W. and TUCKER, R. 1972, *Bilingual Education of Children: The St. Lambert Experiment*. Rowley, Mass.: Newbury House.

LARKIN, R. W. 1970, Pattern maintenance and change in education. *Teachers College Record* 72, 1, 111–19.

LENSKI, G. 1966, *Power and Privilege: A Theory of Social Stratification*. New York: McGraw-Hill.

LIEBERSON, S. 1970, *Language and Ethnic Relations in Canada*. New York: Wiley.

LEIBERSON, S. *et al.* 1975, The course of mother tongue diversity in nations. *American Journal of Sociology* 81, 1, 34–61.

LOMAN, B. 1974, *Språk och Samhälle*. Lund: Gleerups Förlag.

MACKEY, W. F. 1970, A typology of bilingual education. *Foreign Language Annals* 3, 596–608.

—— 1972, *Bilingual Education in a Binational School*. Rowley, Mass.: Newbury House.

MACNAMARA, J. 1972, The objectives of bilingual education in Canada from an English-speaking perspective. In M. SWAIN (ed.) *Bilingual Schooling: Some Experiences in Canada and the United States*. Toronto: Ontario Institute for Studies in Education.

MARIN, P. *et al.* 1975, *The Limits of Schooling*. Englewood Cliffs, NJ: Prentice-Hall.

MEHAN, H. 1972, Language using abilities. *Language Sciences* No. 22.

MELIKOFF, O. 1972, Appendix A: Parents as change agents in education. In W. LAMBERT and R. TUCKER *Bilingual Education of Children*. Rawley, Mass.: Newbury House.

MERTON, R. K. 1957, *Social Theory and Social Structure*. New York: The Free Press.

National Indian Brotherhood 1972, *Indian Control of Indian Education*. Ottawa: 130 Albert Street.

National Institute of Education 1975, Spanish-English bilingual education in the United States: current issues, resources and recommended funding priorities for research. Manuscript.

New York Times 1976a, School in Chicago caters to Indians. June 16, 49.
—— 1976b, Bilingual issue, continued. December 17, A26.
PARSONS, T. 1951, *The Social System*. New York: The Free Press.
—— 1959, The school class as a social system. *Harvard Educational Review* 27.
—— 1961, An outline of the social system. In T. PARSONS, *et al. Theories of Society*. New York: The Free Press.
—— 1964, Evolutionary universals. *American Sociological Review* 29, 339–57.
PASCUAL, H. W. 1976, La educacion bilingüe: retorica y realidad. *Defensa* 4 and 5: 4–7.
PAULSTON, C. B. 1971, On the moral dilemma of the sociolinguist. *Language Learning* 21, 175–81.
—— 1974, Linguistic and communicative competence. *TESOL Quarterly* 8, 4.
—— 1975a, *Implications of Language Learning Theory for Language Planning: Concerns in Bilingual Education*. Arlington, Va.: Center for Applied Linguistics.
—— 1975b, Ethnic relations and bilingual education: accounting for contradictory data. In R. TROIKE and N. MODIANO (eds) *Proceedings of the First Inter-American Conference on Bilingual Education*. Arlington, Va.: Center for Applied Linguistics.
—— 1976a, *Teaching English as a Second Language: Techniques and Procedures*. Cambridge, Mass.: Winthrop. With Mary Bruder.
—— 1976b, Bilingual education and its evaluation: a reaction paper (with comments) to Richard Tucker's 'Cross-Disciplinary Perspectives in Bilingual Education: A Linguistics Review Paper'. Arlington, Va.: Center for Applied Linguistics.
PAULSTON, R. G. 1972, Ethnic revival and educational change in Swedish Lappland. Paper presented at the conference of the American Anthropological Association, Mexico City.
—— 1976, *Conflicting Theories of Social and Educational Change: A Typological Review*. Pittsburgh, Pa.: University Center for International Studies.
PELTO, P. 1970, *Anthropological Research: The Structure of Inquiry*. New York: Harper and Row.
PHILIPS, S. 1970. Acquisition of rules for appropriate speech usage. In J. ALATIS (ed.) *Bilingualism and Language Contact*. 21st Annual Roundtable Georgetown University.
PIALORSI, F. 1974, *Teaching the Bilingual*. Tucson: University of Arizona Press.
PROCHNOW, H. 1973, Final evaluation accomplishment audit of Harlandale independent school district's bilingual education program. ED. 081 1556.
RUSK, B. (ed.) 1971, *Alternatives in Education*. OISE Fifth Anniversary Lectures. Toronto: General Publishing Company.
SÄRKELÄ, T. and KUUSINEN, J. 1975, The connection between the instruction given in one's mothertongue and the ability in languages (title translated). Jyväskylä.
SCHERMERHORN, R. A. 1970, *Comparative Ethnic Relations: A Framework for Theory and Research*. New York: Random House.
SEVILLA-CASAS *et al.* 1973, Addenda of Chicanos and Boricuas to Declaration of Chicago, IX International Congress of Anthropological and Ethnological Sciences. September 7.
SJOBERG, G. and NETT, R. 1968, *Methodology for Social Research*. New York: Harper and Row.
SKUTNABB-KANGAS, T. 1976, Halvspråkighet: ett medel att få invandrarnas barn till löpande bandet? *Invandrare och Minoriteter* 3–4, 31–6.
SKUTNABB-KANGAS, T. and TOUKOMAA, P. 1976, *Teaching Migrant Children's Mothertongue and Learning the Language of the Host Country in the Context*

of the Socio-cultural Situation of the Migrant Family. Helsinki: The Finnish National Commission for UNESCO.

SMELSER, N. J. 1971, *Sociological Theory: A Contemporary View.* New York: General Learning Press.

SPOLSKY, B. (ed.) 1972, *The Language Education of Minority Children.* Rowley, Mass.: Newbury House.

—— 1974a, *American Indian Bilingual Education.* Albuquerque, NM: University of New Mexico Press.

—— 1974b, *A Model for the Description, Analysis, and Perhaps Evaluation of Bilingual Education.* Albuquerque, NM: University of New Mexico Press.

STERN, H. H. 1972, Introduction. In M. SWAIN (ed.) *Bilingual Schooling.* Toronto: OISE.

SWAIN, M. (ed.) 1972, *Bilingual Schooling: Some Experiences in Canada and the United States.* Toronto: Ontario Institute for Studies in Education.

—— 1976a, Evaluation of bilingual education programs: problems and some solutions. Paper presented at the XX Annual Convention of the Comparative and International Education Society, Toronto.

—— 1976b, Bibliography: Research on immersion education for the majority child. *The Canadian Modern Language Review* 32, 5, 592–6.

SWAIN, M. and BRUCK, M. (eds) 1976, Immersion education for the majority child. *The Canadian Modern Language Review* 32, 5.

TUCKER, R. 1976, Summary: Research conference on immersion education for the majority child. In M. SWAIN and M. BRUCK (eds) *Canadian Modern Language Review* 32, 5.

—— 1977, The linguistic perspective. *Bilingual Education: Current Perspectives.* Arlington, Va.: Center for Applied Linguistics.

TURNER, P. R. 1973, *Bilingualism in the Southwest.* Tucson: University of Arizona Press.

US Commission on Civil Rights 1975, *A Better Chance to Learn: Bilingual Bicultural Education.* Washington, DC: US Government Printing Office.

WALLACE, A. 1956, Revitalization movements. *American Anthropologist* 59.

—— 1975, Schools in revolutionary and conservative societies. In F. A. J. IANNI (ed.) *Conflict and Change in Education.* Glenview, Ill.: Scott, Foresman and Company.

WARD, L. 1904, Evolution of social structures. *American Journal of Sociology* 10, 589–605.

Wassaja: A National Newspaper of Indian America 1977, Natives in bilingual education: A disgrace. January.

WHITE, R. 1974, The concept of register and TESL. *TESOL Quarterly* 8, 4.

ZACHARIAH, M. 1975, They who pay the piper call the tune. Paper presented at the Comparative and International Education Society Annual Meeting, March, San Francisco.

ZEITLIN, I. 1968, *Ideology and the Development of Sociological Theory.* Englewood Cliffs, NJ: Prentice-Hall.

5 Biculturalism: Some Reflections and Speculations[1]

Introduction

My colleague Thomas Scovel talks about a phenomenon which he calls 'the hypothesis of professional weakness'. By this term he refers to the occasional tendency one finds in stutterers to become speech pathologists, the slightly loony to become psychiatrists, and childhood weaklings like O. J. Simpson (with rickets) to become professional athletes; in other words, characteristics of the self motivate the choice of professional field. It is exactly such a self-exploratory urge that provided the surface motivation for this paper.[2] More seriously, most of the work I have done during the last few years has been on bilingual education, an educational institution which in the United States is referred to in one breath as bilingual/bicultural education by some. What do they mean by *bicultural?*

There is virtually nothing written on biculturalism. The card catalog at Pitt's Hillman Library has exactly five entries under 'Biculturalism' — all dealing with Anglo-French relations in Canada. Anglo-Canadians are not my idea of an outstanding example of biculturalism, but indeed Webster's definition is perfectly clear: 'the existence of two distinct cultures in one nation'. It seems that we have changed the meaning of the word, but without arriving at any generally agreed on sense.

The way *bicultural* is used in recent dissertations is invariably in the sense of the almost slogan-like 'bilingual/bicultural education programs' where such dissertations typically ignore the bicultural element and rather examine either language proficiency or self-concept. To no surprise, Chicano children in Spanish/English programs show increased self-concept — but the Anglo and Black children do too in such programs (Paulston, 1977) — which leaves me wondering even more just what *bicultural* means.

In this paper I want to consider three questions:

116

(1) Is there, and can there be, such a thing as being bicultural in a fashion similar to which one can be bilingual?

(2) If there is, and it is far from as obvious as one might think, then what is it?

(3) Finally and briefly, what are the implications for the schools, for the universities, for any institutions which deal with members from another culture?

I must point out that these are very elusive topics and I readily admit the speculative nature of my comments. In my readings, I have drawn primarily on anthropology, social psychology and clinical psychiatry, all of which share the problem of soft data. When social psychology does get down to hard data, I find that for my purposes the results become trivial. I have found insightful interpretations along the lines of Seward's (1958) *Clinical Studies in Culture Conflict* and Brislin, Bochner & Lonner's (1975) *Cross-cultural Perspectives on Learning* by far more helpful in sorting out the issues involved.

Just as helpful have been the numerous interviews and discussions I have had with other bicultural individuals, as they have crossed my path during the two, three years this paper has been in the writing. I have been careful not just to introspect and generalize from my own experience because two facts have become clear from these interviews: (1) bicultural individuals do not agree on whether one can be bicultural, and (2) there are different types of bicultural individuals.

Some Considerations of Culture

Definitions are boring, but one cannot very well consider biculturalism without first considering what is meant by culture. Anthropology deals exhaustively with culture and, as we will see, defines it in various ways; but the caution needed is that the emphasis is always on the patterned behavior of the group — not on the behavior of individuals who cross the boundaries of ethnic groups.

Roger Keesing (1974) in 'Theories of culture' reviews the conflicting theories of culture within the discipline of anthropology. He distinguishes between two major paradigms. The first, those theories of culture which see culture as an adaptive system which serves to relate human communities to their ecological settings and cultural change primarily as a process of adaptation and what amounts to natural selection. In order to reach an understanding of biculturalism, such an approach is clearly not fruitful.

The other major paradigm, according to Keesing, includes the ideational theories of culture where culture can be interpreted either as (a) a cognitive system, as inferred ideational codes lying behind the realm of observable events (Goodenough, Frake, Metzger & Williams, Wallace), or as (b) a structural system. Levi-Strauss 'views cultures as shared symbolic systems that are cumulative creations of mind; he seeks to discover in the structuring of cultural domains — myth, art, kinship, language — the principles of mind that generate these cultural elaborations' (Keesing, 1974: 78). (c) Finally there is the view of culture as a symbolic system of shared symbols of meanings:

> More recently, Schneider, has expanded and clarified his conception of culture. Since [his] contrast between 'normative' and 'cultural' levels is conceptually important, it is worth quoting him at greater length as he clarifies it:
>
>> Where the normative system . . . is Ego centered and particularly appropriate to decision-making or interaction models of analysis, culture is system-centered . . . Culture takes man's position vis-a-vis the world rather than a man's position on how to get along in this world as it is given . . . Culture concerns the stage, the stage setting, and the cast of characters; the normative system consists in the stage directions for the actors and how the actors should play their parts on the stage that is so set (Schneider, 1973: 38). (Keesing, 1974: 81)

However theoretically interesting àll this is, it is still not very helpful to our particular problem. In fact, in using most of these theories as a conceptual framework, one would be forced to conclude that logically a person cannot be bicultural. But Keesing goes on to what he calls a conceptual sorting out, where he distinguishes between a cultural and sociocultural system:

> Sociocultural systems represent the social realizations or enactments of ideational designs-for-living in particular environments. A settlement pattern is an element of a sociocultural system, not an element of a cultural system in this sense. (The same conceptual principles might yield densely clustered villages or scattered homesteads, depending on water sources, terrain, arable land, demography, and the peaceful or headhunting predilections of the neighboring tribe.) A mode of subsistence technology similarly is part of a sociocultural system, but not strictly speaking part of a cultural system (people with the same knowledge and set of strategies for subsisting might be primarily horticulturalists in one setting and primarily fishermen in another, might make adzes of flint in one setting or shells in another, might plant taro

on one side of a mountain range or yams on the other side). (Keesing, 1974: 82)

This is beginning to sound very much like *langue* and *parole* and indeed the conceptual untangling Keesing suggests for 'culture' is very familiar to us: he suggests the notion of *cultural competence* as an analog to *linguistic competence:*

> Culture, conceived as a system of competence shared in its broad design and deeper principles, and varying between individuals in its specificities, is then not all of what an individual knows and thinks and feels about his world. It is his theory of what his fellows know, believe, and mean, his theory of the code being followed, the game being played, in the society into which he was born. It is this theory to which a native actor refers in interpreting the unfamiliar or the ambiguous, in interacting with strangers (or supernaturals), and in other settings peripheral to the familiarity of mundane everyday life space; and with which he creates the stage on which the games of life are played. We can account for the individual actor's perception of his culture as external (and as potentially constraining and frustrating); and we can account for the way individuals then can consciously use, manipulate, violate, and try to change what they conceive to be the rules of the game. But note that the actor's 'theory' of his culture, like his theory of his language, may be in large measure unconscious. Actors follow rules of which they are not consciously aware, and assume a world to be 'out there' that they have in fact created with culturally shaped and shaded patterns of mind.
>
> We can recognize that not every individual shares precisely the same theory of the cultural code, that not every individual knows about all sectors of the culture. Thus a cultural description is always an abstracted composite. Depending on the heuristic purposes at hand, we, like the linguists, can plot the distribution of variant versions of competence among subgroups, roles, and individuals. And, like the linguists, we can study the processes of change in conceptual codes as well as in patterns of social behavior. (Keesing, 1974: 89)

One reason for this form of untangling is that it will allow him to deal with the difference between a collective ideational system and the psychodynamics of the individual — a problem which is at the conceptual heart of 'biculturalism'. I will come back to this later because I believe that it is not until we can understand this relationship that we can understand what it means to be bicultural. Keesing goes on to suggest that anthropologists should conceptualise culture as 'cultural competence', only within the wider concern of 'socio-cultural performance'. He concludes:

> Conceiving culture as an ideational subsystem within a vastly complex system, biological, social and symbolic, and grounding our abstract models in the concrete particularities of human social life, should make possible a continuing dialectic that yields deepening understanding. Whether in this quest the concept of culture is progressively refined, radically reinterpreted, or progressively extinguished will in the long run scarcely matter if along the way it has led us to ask strategic questions and to see connections that would otherwise have been hidden. (Keesing, 1974: 94)

I should not at all be surprised if the sort of questions we have to ask about the nature of 'biculturalism' might not contribute to seeing and understanding 'connections that would otherwise have been hidden'.

What one needs to do next is to break down culture learning, i.e. C2 learning, into its component parts to see just what it is you acquire as 'cultural competence'. I shall ultimately argue that a bicultural individual — unlike a bilingual — although he can function with two sets of performances, has in fact only one set of 'cultural competence' and further that this competence is partially eclectic and shows nowhere near the same conformity between individuals as does linguistic competence.

Before I do this, however, I would like to sidetrack in order to mention some aspects of biculturalism or becoming bicultural which I find important, but which do not fit in, orderly — or rather which I cannot fit in orderly — within my framework. Eventually they will have to be fitted in, but for now I will just mention them.

A Digression

Bicultural status seems (almost) always to be gained as a resident in the other country or culture. As I shall discuss later, becoming bicultural is not just a cognitive process which can be carried out apart from the members of the culture. In this aspect becoming bicultural differs from becoming bilingual. It is perfectly possible to learn a foreign language from non-native speakers. As a matter of fact, I never did have an English teacher who was a native speaker. It is also possible to become bilingual without becoming bicultural, while the reverse is not true. Many, naively to my mind, claim that to become bilingual is to become bicultural; but apart from trivialities, this need not follow. Israeli counter intelligence is said to have agents of native Arabic proficiency; yet, who would want to argue that these agents have embraced Arabic culture at any significant level, such as religion and worldview. But bilingual they are.

I myself became fluent in French the years I lived in Morocco, but I certainly did not learn any French culture — those cultural rules I learned were Arabic even through the medium of French or Spanish. As a matter of fact, I disliked the French *colons* in Morocco and their attitudes towards the Arabs and had virtually nothing to do with them. Attitudes and perceptions are enormously important in becoming bicultural, because one does not really emulate behavior one disapproves of, at least not at any deeper level.

Of crucial importance is whether or not the process of becoming bicultural is voluntary or involuntary, whether it represents integration or forced assimilation. The topic surfaced frequently in the interviews, and it is clear that the origin of the contact situation is one reason for the fact that being bicultural means different things to different people.

Consider also the many children born of British parents who grew up in the Commonwealth. They certainly no longer belong in Kenya or the like, but nor do they feel at home in England. 'I just feel that I don't belong anywhere,' said my friend. This odd feeling of belonging nowhere is frequently reported on by people who grew up in a contact situation of two cultures.

Some have used the concept of 'third culture' to deal with the phenomena of 'the cultural patterns created, learned, and shared by members of different societies who are personally involved in relating their societies, or sections thereof, to each other' Useem & Useem, 1967). In other words, in the contact between two cultures, a third culture becomes created, as in the American colony in India with its subgroups of missionaries, businessmen, and government officials, etc. For the purposes of my questions it is not a useful concept, as it lumps together all those factors which I would like to tease apart.

We so emphasize the notion that one culture is not better than another, only different, with the result, I think, that this mind-set obscures the process of becoming bicultural. When I lived and taught in a small rural town of some 300 families in southern Minnesota, I was always odd man out — and eventually came to accept at some subliminal level that there must be something wrong with me. And of all unlikely places, I found my bearings again in Tangier, where I felt in a sense like coming home. Tangier of course was nothing like Sweden, but it had a fairly large cosmopolitan European settlement and it was easier for me to relate to them than to puritan Minnesota.

At this level it is not true that one culture is not better, or rather, perceived as better, than another — the selection of cultural traits is based on evaluation.

Becoming Bicultural

Everett Kleinjans (1975) suggests a model for learning a second culture in his 'A Question of Ethics' which provides a framework for thinking about the dimensions of (not *how* but) *what* we learn in learning a C2. The model has three categories: *cognition, affection* and *action,* and each domain has a number of levels from superficial down to profound.

Under *Cognition,* we find: information, analysis, synthesis, comprehension, insight. Cognition deals with knowing the what and why about another culture and can partially be learned outside the culture itself. Briefly, *information* deals with encyclopedia type facts; person, places, events, dates, sort of thing. (Cf. the bicultural component of the bilingual programs.) *Analysis* separates out the parts of the culture like family system, educational process, religion, art, language, etc., while *synthesis* integrates the meaningful relationship of the parts. Whereas synthesis deals with facts or existing elements, *comprehension* deals with new items 'with anticipation, extrapolation, and prediction'.

This sort of knowledge *about* other cultures is enormously important for people like us who constantly deal with persons from other cultures. Let me give you some examples. In the English Language Institute, we had a Saudi student who because of poor work, excessive absences and attitude was not allowed, according to Institute rules which he knew well, to register for the next term. Mary Bruder, our Associate Director, came to see me. 'Throw him out,' said I. 'But he promised,' said Mary. I suppose I said something like 'promises schmomises'. But Mary pointed out to me — who should have known — that when they, Arabs, promise, they usually keep their promise. So the young man was called into my office, duly raked over the coals while he pitiously, and I must admit, charmingly, promised all the while. 'If you had our book here,' he said. 'It's all right,' said I most seriously, 'you may promise to Allah.' So the young man, eyes heavenward with lifted hand swore to reform his errant ways. He also signed a most solemn written agreement/promise, which Mary had composed for the occasion. My guess is that our prediction that he will shape up is accurate.[3]

Another example concerns a Peruvian student from Puno, a Quechua Indian who came to see me because he was feeling sick and nauseated, could not sleep and in fact wanted to go home, an enormous sacrifice on his part since he had a full scholarship at an American university, the chance of a lifetime. Now, Quechuas distinguish between somatic and psychosomatic illnesses, and for the latter they seek the help not of a physician but of a *curandera,* who cures by mildly magical rituals. I checked to see whether he had seen a physician which he had. 'Well,' I said, 'what you need is a *curandera,* not me,' and went on to explain to him the symptoms of culture shock. As he looked at me wide-eyed, I explained that in all likelihood at least two-thirds of his group were going through the same symptoms he had. When I added that probably he also found the food terrible and that he sorely missed rice with his meals, he clearly thought I was clairvoyant if not a *curandera.* I forebore to mention that every student we have ever had from rice-eating cultures has had that complaint. When he realized that his symptoms really were normal for his situation he went away smiling, saying 'Doctora, we have a saying that suffering is the "salsa de la vida"'. The next time I heard about him was after his first term at his university where he had amassed the respectable QPA of 3.57. Clearly, not only is it useful for us to know about other cultural rules, it also is helpful to the people we deal with.

Finally, by *insight* Kleinjans means the ability to not only look at a culture from the inside but to see the world outside as the people of that culture see it. When I told Mary about the Saudi promising to Allah we both smiled, partially I suppose out of goodwill, but more because — although at the time it was a most appropriate Arabic thing to do — it struck me, at least, as a very un-American thing to do; to call your student in and make him promise to God that he will do his homework on time just isn't the thing American professors are supposed to do. It is probably unconstitutional.

But this ability to look at the same phenomenon, or rather to be able to interpret what the same phenomenon means from the viewpoint of two cultures, I think is a hallmark of the bicultural individual. My husband sometimes says, 'What would your parents say if they saw you now?' and it is exactly this kind of bi-focal view he has in mind. Although my behavior is socially appropriate as far as he is concerned, he is teasing me for deviant behavior according to Swedish rules.

But note that all of this has only to do with the head, so to speak; none of it has anything to do with the attitudes and feelings people have towards other cultures.

Under the *Affection* domain, Kleinjans posits the following levels: perception, appreciation, reevaluation, reorientation, identification. *Perception* and *appreciation* simply refer to the coming to know and to like aspects of another culture, like food and music as well as aesthetic and moral values. It is hard for me now to think that Arabic music once just sounded like awful noise or that I thought Peruvian food was awful. Over time I learned to appreciate both. I eventually also learned to function with a different system of time but I rarely appreciated it. It is, at superficial behavior levels, perfectly possible to understand and even to be able to behave in ways one still dislikes.

Reevaluation is the process of changing one's values. 'It might mean a shift in priorities, the giving up of certain values for new ones, or an enlargement of one's value system.' *Reorientation* means changing the direction of one's life, 'spurred by values he has adopted from the second culture'. *Identification* is becoming one with the people of the other culture; 'A person changes citizenship'. At these levels I don't believe it is possible to be bicultural. When I took out US citizenship, I had to give up my Swedish citizenship; I could not have both. And so it is with conflicting cultural values; in the same way as one just can't believe in the overriding importance of consensus and conciliation of group interests at the same time as one believes in confrontation and the overriding rights of the individual in solving problems.

So what happens, I think, is that the individual picks and chooses. Some aspects of culture are beyond modification. Many Americans comment on my frankness, but Swedes never do. Now I wouldn't want to claim that Swedes lie less than Americans, but I do think there is more emphasis on the value of always telling the truth (or saying nothing) in the socialization process of Swedish children. I know some people dislike me for it, and still I don't change because I simply cannot. But many aspects of culture are within the bounds of modification; one can learn to be half an hour late and not consider it moral slackness; one can learn to eat with one's fingers and still feel like an adult. But such modifications mainly concern surface behavior, behavior one can switch back and forth.

Now, to my mind, one of the major questions which remains to be dealt with is the process of acquiring a 'cultural competence' which is based on two cultural systems. Are some patterns more salient than others, are some reinforcements stronger than others, are some values more inherently right than others?

We can find some directions for beginning to think about this problem in at first glance an unlikely source: Robert Edgerton's (1976) monograph *Deviance: A Cross-Cultural Perspective*. Now I am most specifically not claiming that being bicultural is deviant behavior, but I wonder if some of the same processes involved in deviant behavior may not also be involved in becoming bicultural.

To wit. Edgerton who is Professor of Anthropology in the Department of Psychiatry at UCLA, in his very carefully reasoned work discusses the difficulty anthropology has had in accounting for deviant behavior. All societies have cultural rules for appropriate behavior, yet all people misbehave. True, what is appropriate behavior in one culture is deviant behavior in another and vice versa; yet, all people misbehave and some more than others. Why? After a review of various theories which seek to explain deviance (social strain theory; subcultural conflict theory; psychological defense or commitment; biological defect; human nature), Edgerton considers the data of deviance from a cross-cultural perspective; data which need not concern us here, however fascinating it is. His attempt to link temperament and deviance does, however.

Individuality of temperament is a genetic predisposition to react to an environment in certain ways. Temperament as such is largely unyielding to cultural pressure, and he draws on the work of Thomas, Chess & Birch (1968) in this formulation. People *are* born with varying patterns of temperament, and these *are* relatively difficult to change. He goes on to say that societies therefore, can easily choose to define some children as bad and others as good, and he goes on to discuss deviance. But it should be equally true that individuals who are given a chance to pick and choose between two cultural systems can equally easily choose to define some cultural traits as good and some as bad and pick accordingly. I am sure that is what I have done. But what I like and dislike does not conform to any one culture; it is an idiosyncratic mixture of Swedish and American 'cultural competence' even though I am capable of appropriate 'socio-cultural performance', in Keesing's terms, in both cultures.

I think one thing that happens with or in bicultural eclecticism is that the bicultural individual becomes more impervious to sanctions he does not like (I am not absolutely sure about this, but many of the informants also said this was how they felt). For example, when a Latin American colleague tells me that I am being anal compulsive about time, I just shrug off the comment and claim Swedish status. But that does not stop me at all, when my mother hurries me because I am five minutes late, from informing her that Swedes are guilt-ridden, super-ego bound, hysterical about time, and claim American status.

An obvious difference between bilingualism and biculturalism is that when you speak Swedish or English, it is perfectly obvious which set of rules you are drawing on. But with behavior it is not necessarily clear just which cultural system your performance rules belong to. This can be a cause for problem, especially with very fluent speakers, as the addressee will fail to recognize another cultural system at work and instead merely see deviant behavior. As Virginia Allen has pointed out, it may be quite useful to keep a foreign accent.

Sometimes behavior may be deviant to both cultural systems. Occasionally on the street, by the bus stop next to my department, there are some black schoolboys who beg money for bus fare. Their mothers would have their hide, if they only knew, but friendly whites exclaim over black social conditions and pay off their collective guilt with a quarter. The boys' behavior is deviant to both cultures; the boys, however, accurately bank on whites' ignorance of acceptable black behavior and so run their game successfully. I suspect most bicultural individuals, consciously or not, occasionally run the same sort of game where the individual claims status of the other culture when in fact his behavior is highly idiosyncratic and outside both his ideational cultural systems.

Sometimes it happens that the individual is not allowed to pick and choose between his two cultures but will have conflicting values imposed on him. The result is often some form of psychopathology. Seward (1958) in her fascinating collection of case studies documents the stress of such individuals, like the Japanese Nisei boy torn between his desire to espouse modern egalitarian values and the imposition of his father's strictly traditional Japanese values. His response to such conflict was mental breakdown, the inability (refusal?) to function with *any* cultural rules.

Implications for Education

In language teaching we are increasingly making the distinction between our teaching and the students' learning, with the emphasis on the latter. This dichotomy becomes very obvious when one is talking about biculturalism. Culture can be taught only at a cognitive level. Such information is important especially for foreign students studying in the United States. Teaching culture at this level may seem trivial, like our telling the Muslim students that as long as they buy kosher meat they need not worry about pork, but learning such rules reduces anxiety and culture shock. Such rules carry the advantage that the learning of them rarely entails approval or endorsement which is not true of cultural rules or patterns in the affective domain. Foreign students are sensitive to having foreign values imposed on them while they usually don't mind learning 'local' eccentricities which is of course how others' rules strike one. Learning cultural trivia-rules is learning to get around in another culture.

An important aspect of culture which falls under the cognitive domain is learning sociolinguistic rules or what Hymes (1972) calls 'communicative competence', the appropriate (to the target culture) social use of language. For example, it is not enough to teach the Japanese wh-questions like 'How old is your daughter?' They also need to learn that it is not appropriate to ask, as I was asked a few years ago, 'How old are you to have been promoted to Associate Professor?' (Paulston, 1974).

In bilingual/bicultural education the referent of 'bicultural' is almost invariably the mother tongue culture, the culture the children already know. One is reminded of Lado's (1957) parodical stereotype of 'Mexicans end-lessly dancing around a hat' when one sees the superficial cognitive levels which passes for bicultural teaching. 'At the end of this lesson, the children will be able to correctly identify the Mexican flag' is a verbatim quotation from such a curriculum which purports to be bicultural. Apart from the confusion of nationalism with culture, the teaching of such facile, non-func-tional facts under the guise of 'bicultural' merely becomes a deterrant in such programs where the goals rather should be an affirmation of native values and a positive attitude towards the home culture. It should also be clear that any support of culture learning or culture maintenance in the affective domain necessitates teachers who are members of the same home culture as the children, not just bilingual in the home tongue and English.

But by the time children come to school they have already internalized a great deal of the home culture and what they very much need, if they are to succeed in school, is to learn the cultural ways of mainstream America. Susan Philips (1970) discusses this problem in her work on the Warm Springs Indian Reservation for which she uses Hymes' notion of communicative competence in accounting for the children's school failure. The children's native ways of speaking and strategies for learning are very different from those of the Anglo school's, consequently, 'Indian children fail to partici-pate verbally in the classroom interaction because the social conditions for participation to which they have become accustomed in the Indian com-munity are lacking'.

Educators cannot assume that because Indian children (or children from other cultural backgrounds than that which is implicit in Ameri-can classrooms) speak English, or are taught it in school, that they have also assimilated all of the sociolinguistic rules underlying inter-action in classrooms and other non-Indian social situations where English is spoken. (Philips, 1970: 95)

I think today most bilingual program personnel make no such assumption, but rather they assume that the teacher will adjust his ways, and so culture interference in the classroom will be minimized. This is exactly what some of the teachers whom Philips observed did; they adjusted their teaching to ways appropriate to Indian culture. But the ultimate result was not what they had expected. It was the very students with teachers sensitive to Indian cultures who were the first to fail out once they went to school off the reservation; this situation leads Philips to comment that:

> The teachers who make these adjustments, and not all do, are sensitive to the inclinations of their students and want to teach them through means to which they most readily adapt. However, by doing so, they are avoiding teaching the Indian children how to communicate in precisely those contexts in which they are least able, and most need to learn how to communicate if they are to do well in school. (Philips 1970: 88)

She ends her paper by saying that the children must be taught 'the rules for appropriate speech usage', i.e. that they must be taught the ways of speaking, acceptable to the dominant culture. As we have seen, beyond a superficial level, culture learning entails firsthand exposure to members of the C2, and it follows, however unpalatable some will find this statement, that the children must have access to Anglo teachers, if they are to learn the rules of mainstream culture. It will be the students' choice what aspects, if any, of mainstream culture they care to incorporate into their bicultural make-up, and no school or curriculum can dictate that choice. But to deny them the opportunity of choice I find reprehensible.

It is this same opportunity of choice which necessitates not only Anglo teachers but also the home culture component in a truly bilingual/bicultural program in order to avoid the wholesale imposition of the second culture's values which occasionally results in pathology of the kind Seward discusses. Students in the public schools who are members of ethnic minority groups in the United States will have been exposed, albeit in varying degrees, to American mainstream culture all their lives. They will learn to become bicultural and they will suit themselves in the doing of it. We may say 'How typically Mexican', or 'How very Puerto Rican', but we never say 'How very typically Puerto Rican-North American bicultural behavior' for the simple reason that being bicultural is an individual matter which does not lend itself to stereotyping. Nor can it be taught. Becoming bicultural is an eclectic process, and what a bicultural program should hope to do is to allow the student the right to pick and choose his own individual make-up as a bicultural person from the two cultures and the members of those cultures he is exposed to in the school.

Notes

1. This article is the written version of my TESOL presidential address in Miami, 1977. I have deliberately kept the somewhat chatty style of the original in order to underscore the speculative, non-scholarly nature of the paper. I owe thanks to the many individuals who have shared with me their own introspections and insights into the nature of biculturalism; without their contributions I could not have written the paper.
2. The following information is relevant for interpreting my comments. I was born and grew up in Sweden until I was 18 at which time I came to the United States, of which country I am now a citizen. Subsequent to 1960, I have spent some seven years living abroad in Morocco, India, Peru as well as in Sweden.
3. As this article goes to print, I reluctantly submit the following addenda. Our prediction was wrong, but not for the expected reasons. The young man subsequently succumbed to emotional distress which incapacitated him for the serious work intensive language learning is. Three of his colleagues did pull through, similarly given a second chance. The episode also illustates how difficult it is to identify incipient disturbance cross-culturally.

Bibliography

BOCK, P. (ed.) 1970, *Culture Shock: A Reader in Modern Cultural Anthropology.* New York: Alfred Knopf.
BRISLIN, R. W. (ed.) 1978, *Culture Learning.* Honolulu, Hawaii: University Press of Hawaii.
BRISLIN, R. W., BOCHNER, S. and LONNER, W. J. (eds) 1975, *Cross-Cultural Perspectives on Learning.* New York: John Wiley & Sons.
EBEL, C. 1977, Can one be bilingual and not be bicultural? *BESL Reporter* 3, 1, 5–6.
EDGERTON, R. B. 1973, *Deviant Behavior and Cultural Theory.* Module in Anthropology, No. 37. Menlo Park, California: Addison-Wesley.
—— 1976, *Deviance: A Cross-Cultural Perspective.* Menlo Park, California: Cummings Publishing Co.
GORDON, R. L. 1975, *Living in Latin America: A Case Study in Cross-Cultural Communication.* Skokie, Illinois: National Textbook Co.
HYMES, D. 1972, On communicative competence. In J. B. PRIDE and J. HOLMES (eds) *Sociolinguistics.* Harmondsworth, England: Penguin Books.
KEESING, R. 1974, Theories of culture. In B. SIEGEL (ed.) *Annual Review of Anthropology*, Vol. 3 (pp. 73–97). Palo Alto, California.
KLEINJANS, E. 1975, A question of ethics. *Exchange* X, 4, 20–5.
LADO, R. 1957, *Linguistics Across Cultures.* Ann Arbor: University of Michigan Press.
OSGOOD, C. E., MAY, W. H. and MIRON, M. S. 1975, *Cross-Cultural Universals of Affective Meaning.* Urbana, Illinois: University of Illinois Press.
PAULSTON, C. B. 1974, Linguistic and communicative competence. *TESOL Quarterly* 8, 4.
—— 1977, Research. *Bilingual Education: Current Perspectives — Linguistics.* Arlington, Virginia: Center for Applied Linguistics.

PHILIPS, S. 1970, Acquisition of rules for appropriate speech usage. In J. ALATIS (ed.) *Bilingualism and Language Contact.* 21st Annual Roundtable, Georgetown University.

SAVILLE-TROIKE, M. 1976, On bilingualism and biculturalism in education. Paper presented at the Symposium on Language Development in a Bilingual Setting, Los Angeles, California.

SCHNEIDER, L. and BONJEAN, C. M. (eds) 1973, *The Idea of Culture in the Social Sciences.* Cambridge: University Press.

SEELYE, N. 1976, *Teaching Culture.* Skokie, Illinois: National Textbook Co.

SEWARD, G. 1958, *Clinical Studies in Culture Conflict.* New York: The Ronald Press Co.

SMALLEY, W. A. 1963, Culture shock, language shock, and the shock of self-discovery. *Practical Anthropology* 10, 2.

STEWART, E. C. 1971, *American Cultural Patterns: A Cross-Cultural Perspective.* Pittsburgh, Pennsylvania: Regional Council for International Education.

THOMAS, E. M., CHESS, S. and BIRCH, H. 1968, *Temperament and Behavior Disorders in Children.* New York: Holt, Rinehart and Winston.

Topics in Culture Learning, Vol. 1973 — East–West Center, East–West Culture Learning Institute, Honolulu, Hawaii.

USEEM, J. and USEEM, R. 1967, The interfaces of a binational third culture: A study of the American community in India. *Journal of Social Issues* 23, 1, 130–43.

6 Quantitative and Qualitative Research on Bilingual Education in the United States

'Then how long will it last, this love?' (in jest)
'I don't know.'
'Three weeks, three years, three decades . . . ?'
'You are like all the others . . . trying to *shorten eternity* with numbers.' (spoken quietly, but with intense feeling)

from Lawrence Durrell, *Justine*

Most research on bilingual education has dealt with quantitative variables within a structural-functionist approach. Since many of the concerns which motivate the research on bilingual education are inherently those of a conflict theory approach, it is not surprising to find an increasing dissatisfaction with the traditional quantificational mode of research. I do not intend this presentation to be a scholarly paper but rather reflections and reportage, drawing on National Institute of Education proposals and planning papers, unpublished papers and discussions with colleagues. To say that this is not a scholarly paper is not to belittle the importance of the topic; I do think the direction toward qualitative research on bilingual education is the most important development I have seen during the last ten years.

Thomas Kuhn (1971) in his seminal *The Structure of Scientific Revolutions* posits the notion of paradigm shift. By paradigms Kuhn means the way a scientific community views a field of study, identifies appropriate problems for study, and specifies legitimate concepts and methods. The literature and research which question the exclusivity of quantitative methodologies in educational research frequently draw on Kuhn for key concepts, and I have found it useful in examining the at times contradictory findings on bilingual education. R. G. Paulston (1976), drawing on the literature of social and educational change, posits two major paradigms: the functional or 'equilibrium' paradigm, and the conflict paradigm. Theories (which admittedly cross and overlap) which fall within the equilibrium paradigm are evolutionary and neo-evolutionary, structural-functionist, and system analysis. Basically they are all concerned with maintaining society in an equilibrium through the harmonious relationship of the social components, and they emphasize smooth, cumulative change. The key concept for education programs is *efficiency,* and it is through arguments of increased efficiency that bilingual education is advocated, evaluated, and defended.

Theoretical approaches which fall within the conflict paradigm are group conflict theory, cultural revitalization theory, and an anarchistic-utopian approach. These theories emphasize the inherent instability of social systems and the consequent conflict over values, resources, and power. The definition of *the* problem of bilingual education from a conflict perspective is no longer the functionist 'unequal opportunity' but rather one of structured inequity, of 'persistence of poverty, intractability of inequality of incomes and inequality of economic and social opportunity' (Bowles, Gintis & Meyer, 1976). Unequal opportunity, the existence of which is certainly not denied, tends to be seen as a result of a condition of inequity rather than as a cause of school failure. Consequently in conflict oriented studies the solutions to educational problems are rarely sought in terms of techno-cractic efficiency; the emphasis is on *equity.* This necessarily leads to disagreement over the evaluation of bilingual education programs. (For a detailed discussion, see C. B. Paulston, 1980, or Chapter 4, this volume.)

I admit that my own bias tends toward a worldview of the conflict paradigm, but I do not wish to give the impression that a conflict perspective is the most fruitful approach to all questions in bilingual education. Clearly what is needed is a dialectic, a working out which questions within the field of bilingual education are most fruitfully approached from a structural-functionist approach and which are best approached from a conflict perspective. Sometimes the same problem can be approached from both perspectives: dealing with the issue of teacher qualifications, ESL (English as a Second Language) proponents argue for Anglo teachers, i.e. native speakers of English, in terms of efficient teaching while bilingual education proponents argue for minority teachers in terms of ethnic group belongingness. Such diverse answers can be seen to clarify not only the questions and the underlying assumptions but also to identify additional variables to consider in the research design. The evaluation research of the Canadian immersion programs typically never considers teacher ethnicity as a variable and that is in itself important information — if you happen to notice it.

Parallel to these discussions on theoretical approaches in the literature on social and educational change, the last decade has seen an increasingly concerned debate on quantitative versus qualitative approaches to educational research. One of the best sources for an introduction is Cook & Reichardt (1979), *Qualitative and Quantitative Methods in Evaluation Research*, with its many excellent references. They define quantitative methods as 'techniques of randomized experiments, quasi-experiments, paper and pencil "objective" tests, multivariate statistical analyses, sample surveys, and the like' in contrast to qualitative methods which include 'ethnography, case studies, in-depth interviews, and participant-observation' (Cook & Reichardt, 1979: 7) As Rist (1977: 42) points out, 'quantitative research is *the* dominant methodology in educational research'. Many cite Campbell & Stanley (1963) from their widely used textbook: 'the only available route to cumulative progress' (p. 3), and their view on experimental design as 'the only means for settling disputes regarding educational practice, the only way of verifying educational improvements, and the only way of establishing a cumulative tradition in which improvements can be introduced without the danger of a faddish discard of old wisdom in favor of inferior novelties' (p. 2). This methodology is seen as derived from the natural sciences:

> Human events are assumed to be lawful; man and his creations are part of the natural world. The development, elaboration, and verification of generalizations about the natural world become the first task of the researcher. (Rist, 1977: 42)

And this is of course the problem. Man's behavior is not always lawful, and the argument against standard quantitative methodology is that it is not enough to *know*, one must also *understand* the inner perspective of human behavior; the difference between *wissen* and *verstehen*. Rist (1977: 44) again: 'Qualitative research is predicated upon the assumption that this method of "inner understanding" enables a comprehension of human behavior in greater depth than is possible from the study of surface behavior, the focus of quantitative methodologies'. The basic difference between the two methods is that the quantitative approach begins with models and hypotheses and predetermined variables while the 'qualitative methodology allows the researcher "to get close to the data", thereby developing the analytical, conceptual, and categorical components of explanation from the data itself' (Filstead, 1970: 6).

An example comes from my own fieldwork on Catalan language maintenance. I had proposed to investigate the continued use of Catalan in Spain as a function of ethnic group boundary maintenance (Barth, 1969). It was a neat proposal, only it was wrong. Halfway through, during some interviews, I began the discovery that Catalunya is a matter of nationalism, not ethnicity. This discovery invalidated the use of the theoretical framework and attempted explanations. It still frightens me how easily I could have missed such data, and the point I am making here is that nothing short of living in Barcelona, of participant-observation, of getting close to the data could have allowed me this insight and shown me the necessity to reconceptualize my categories. It is a typical pro-qualitative methodology argument.

Filstead sums up the comparison between the two approaches, cast as many of the discussions are in Kuhn's terms of paradigms and paradigm clash:[1]

> In sum, the quantitative paradigm employs a lock-step model of logico-deductive reasoning from theory to propositions, concept formation, operational definition, measurement of the operational definitions, data collection, hypothesis testing, and analysis. The qualitative paradigm is a dynamic interchange between theory, concepts, and data with constant feedback and modifications of theory and concepts based on the data collected. This emerging, refined 'explanation framework' gives direction to where additional data need to be collected. It is marked by a concern with the discovery of theory rather than the verification of theory. (Filstead, 1979: 38)

Now, the interesting thing is that virtually all structural/functionist research on bilingual education is quantitative. Within the conflict theory perspective there are exceptions, such as Toukomaa's quantitative work which is clearly neo-marxist[2] in value orientation, but all qualitative research on bilingual education or applicable to bilingual education can be classified as belonging to a conflict perspective. Why this is so, I do not know. As R. G. Paulston (1979: 27) points out: 'The relationships between a choice of theoretical framework and choice of appropriate methodology is all too little studied.' At this point I can only speculate.

Most research on bilingual education is evaluation research. Such research claims to draw on all available disciplines but in fact draws primarily on the behavioral sciences with an occasional sorti into sociology. These fields typically deal with research on predetermined variables which are operationalized and measured. In bilingual education, reading scores, vocabulary tests and related matters of language proficiency also easily lend themselves to quantification[3] and research designs with treatment variables. The standard quantitative research design is easily applicable.

Recently, however, there has been an emphasis not only on two languages in the classroom but also on the cultures in contact, and in the United States bilingual education is often referred to as bilingual/bicultural education. Ethnography does not deal with predetermined variables, and key concepts in the study of culture, culture conflict and assimilation do not easily lend themselves to quantification. The point I am making is that although the literature on the dichotomy of quantitative and qualitative methods in evaluation research avoids any explanatory mention of the disciplines and their preferred mode of investigation, it seems undeniable to me that there is a close link between research question, method of investigation and the particular discipline of the researcher. This is all to the good, I think, in our concern with research methods. While choice of question is clearly tied to paradigm and world view, methods need not be except by historical accident of training and expertise. Give a small boy a hammer and everything he encounters needs hammering, in Kaplan's terms. We often do research the way we were trained without any moral sense of commitment. We are more willing to learn new ways of data collection and analysis than we are of changing our view of the world.

Let me illustrate. During my tenure on a Research Grants Committee, I recall a proposal which posited a research design where the treatment consisted of a program where Black mothers were instructed in 'proper interaction' with their young children. The underlying rationale was that Black children fail in school because they have faulty language because their mothers don't know how to interact with them. As a linguist I know that Black children have anything but faulty language, and I rejected the problem formulation. As me, I found the thought ludicrous that mothers wouldn't know how to interact with their children. Most of all, I was indignant over the kind of value formulation which would lead to this kind of formalized attempt at cultural interference and pressure for assimilation into ways of the superordinate group (vocabulary marked for a conflict perspective, incidentally). The methodology of the proposal, I recall, was impeccable and I had no technical objections. Interestingly enough, I think it was my moral indignation rather than technical linguistic objections that was most effective in convincing the rest of the committee that the proposal did not merit funding. The point is that research methodology in its narrow sense is nowhere near as political and moral as the way we look at the world and the questions we ask.

The two, worldview and methodology, often get confused in the literature on bilingual education where one is argued in terms of the other. The issues of *Invandrare och Minoriteter* (Ekstrand, 1980; Hanson, 1980; Skutnabb-Kangas, 1980) give us a representative example in the Ekstrand/ Hanson/Skutnabb-Kangas debate. Ekstrand argues from a classical structural-functional perspective on the basis of quantitative data for his point on mother tongue classes and transitional models. Much of what he says is common sense if you believe that the function of bilingual education is efficient teaching of the superordinate language and a mechanism for rapid assimilation of ethnic groups. From our viewpoint the interesting thing is that he dismisses contradictory data with claims upon the canons of quantitative methodology: 'It is even unlikely that so little data could give any valid foundation for conclusions' (Ekstrand, 1980: 20, my translation). I think of 'Case #1. Miss Anna O' and read on. I have the strong feeling from reading Ekstrand that he is defending his own view of the world and that he sees issues of research methodology as the best defense. It is convenient in that it assures that any data, not of his choosing, is not acceptable.

Hanson (1980) most wisely refuses the bait and instead rejects Ekstrand's world view: 'Mothertongue classes do not aim "directly" for bilingualism. They aim primarily to make the children feel secure in their schoolwork. When children feel secure, they can do work in school. They can then among other things learn two languages' (my translation). No canons of research methodology can refute Hanson's view of the objectives of bilingual education; at most one can question whether it coincides with the legal Swedish position. Whether it does or not will not change Hanson's view; we do not need data and evidence from research to reject someone's worldview.

It is not coincidental that Hanson's key point of 'security' is difficult to operationalize and measure on a paper and pencil objective test without trivializing the concept. Does that make it any less important? A key objection to exclusively quantitative research is the consequence that if you can't measure a concept, it doesn't exist. Incidentally, self concept is marginally related to 'security', and in the American studies, childrens' scores on self concept increased in the bilingual program, not only for the Hispanic children but also for the Anglo and Black children. I know the scores but without additional qualitative data I cannot understand why this is so. Perhaps the children felt secure.

Hanson really does not deal with data but bases his argument on judgment and simply appeals to the reader to choose whose judgment is the sounder. If we only admitted it more often, this is what all research, quantitative and qualitative, eventually comes to. Skutnabb-Kangas (1980) does give us data, beautiful qualitative data in the form of essays and poems written by immigrants. They are introduced by a paragraph which exemplifies the dichotomy between the qualitative and quantitative methods:

> Lars Henric Ekstrand claims that Jim Cummins 'must make more precise exactly what it is that makes the mother tongue so special'

(Ekstrand, 1980: 20). It is a question only monolingual stupidity can make. She/he who only has one language, she/he who has never had his/her language seriously threatened, perhaps she/he can have such an unreflecting and unconscious understanding of what his/her language means. I shall once again quote an immigrant. (Skutnabb-Kangas, 1980: 11, my translation)

No one can question the validity of Javala's feelings in the moving paragraphs which follow. What is questioned in the literature is the reliability of qualitative data, i.e. how representative is Javala's experience of the other Finnish immigrants?

I have digressed at this length in order to illustrate how differences in ways of defining problems in bilingual education research, often based on political and moral values, then become discussed in terms of research methodology, and mostly covertly so. Since it is unlikely that either Ekstrand or Skutnabb-Kangas will be swayed from their positions by the other's argument, one wonders if this sort of debate stirs anything except hard feelings. I think so, maybe because I would like to think so.

He who pays the piper, calls the tune. A very large amount if not most evaluation research on bilingual education is funded by outside sources, here as well as in Sweden. I would like to think that such debates demonstrate to those in charge of allocating funds for research that (1) you can be very subjective with quantitative research and that (2) there are alternative questions to be asked and other ways of thinking about data. This has been the case in the United States. Since the so-called Bilingual Education Act of 1968, increasingly large amounts of federal monies have been spent on bilingual education, to the sum of 150 million dollars last fiscal year. Congress has now mandated a large scale research study, which will form the basis for a report to Congress in 1981, when the case for bilingual education will be reevaluated (NIE, 1980a). Five million children is after all a sizeable number of children to be concerned about (NIE, 1980b). The basic arguments for the original legislation were those of efficiency: non-English speaking children would learn English better in bilingual programs than in the traditional English monolingual programs. Now, more than ten years later, there is very little hard evidence to support such a claim: 'Furthermore, the reported results have been mostly negative or neutral' (Goodrich, 1980: 2). Everyone concerned about bilingual education wonders at this point what the future will hold.

Filstead (1979), in his discussion of the evaluation of the 'Great Society Programs', writes:

The quantitative model was looked upon as the only way to definitively know the (already assumed) positive impact of such programs.

Given this climate, it is little wonder that so much allegiance was given this approach to program evaluation. Consequently, where the outcomes of these evaluations were ambiguous, or, worse, negative, and the mode and style of feedback difficult and at times impossible to comprehend, a sense of disenchantment with these approaches started to develop . . . With the result of many social interventions yielding unclear or negative impacts, bureaucrats began to distrust such evaluation approaches because they did not have potential benefit to their organizations. Furthermore, underlying these concerns was a growing belief that these types of quantitative evaluations really did not capture the 'experience' or the 'essence' of the intervention program under study. That is to say, program administrators often felt the evaluation effort achieved only an incomplete comprehension of the social intervention. (Filstead, 1979: 40)

From the outside, it is difficult to ascribe motives to the National Institute of Education (NIE), who was asked to coordinate the Congress-mandated study, but whatever the reasons, in the Request for Proposals, they specifically asked for 'an examination of ways to merge qualitative and quantitative information' (Goodrich, 1980: 21) and Goodrich (1980: 2) writes in that same NIE Planning Paper: 'It seems essential to avoid the large scale research study that, because of its exclusive reliance on the quantitative paradigm, is likely to miss the positive effects of bilingual education.' My guess is that most proponents/researchers this time around assume that evidence for bilingual education which is (1) real, deep, and of inner understanding and (2) positive is most likely to be reached through qualitative means.

Goodrich charts the attributes of the qualitative and quantitative approaches (see Table 6.1), which he perceives to be at the paradigmatic level, and goes on to discuss these issues.

In particular I want to cite his discussion of the Berliner & Tikunoff (1976) study as it gives an idea of the proposed lines of research.

They attempted in the BTES study to combine quantitative and qualitative methodologies. They wished to identify variables across which more and less effective classrooms vary without constraining the investigation by using any of the traditionally oriented observation instruments. To do this they developed a list of instructional dimensions by ethnographic means. Ten more and ten less effective teachers were

TABLE 6.1   *Attributes of the qualitative and quantitative paradigms**

Qualitative paradigm	Quantitative paradigm
Advocates the use of qualitative methods.	Advocates the use of quantitative methods.
Phenomenologism; 'concerned with understanding human behavior from the actor's own frame of reference'.	Logical-positivism; 'seeks the *facts* or *causes* of social phenomena with little regard for the subjective states of individuals'.
Naturalistic and uncontrolled observation. Assumes a dynamic reality.	Obtrusive and controlled measurement. Assumes a stable reality.
Subjective.	Objective.
Close to the data; the 'insider' perspective. Valid; 'real', 'rich', and 'deep'.	Removed from the data; the 'outsider' perspective. Reliable; 'hard', and replicable data.
Grounded, discovery-oriented, exploratory, expansionist, descriptive, and inductive.	Ungrounded, verification-oriented, confirmatory, reductionist, inferential and hypothetico-deductive.
Process-oriented.	Outcome-oriented.
Valid; 'real', 'rich', and 'deep' data.	Reliable; 'hard', and replicable data.
Ungeneralizable; small samples or single case studies.	Generalizable; large samples.

*This table is adapted from Cook & Reichardt (1979). Some attributes have been combined and others discarded in an attempt to reduce overlapping. (Goodrich, 1980: 22) identified by examining gain scores of tests addressed directly to two week Experimental Teaching Units (ETU's). Ethnographers observed these classes (without knowledge of which were effective and which not) and prepared prose ethnographic protocols describing classroom behaviors. The protocols were paired (more versus less effective) and analyzed for variables, concepts, or dimensions that described inter-classroom variations. The very large initial list was pared to 61 mostly non-overlapping variables. These were then instrumented via rating scales, validated by reexamination of the original protocols. This technique combines phenomenological and logical-positive approaches effectively. It begins with an open, atheo-retical, observation that excludes little, and proceeds to scales that can be used in quantitative analyses.

The BTES approach is a particular example of using phenomeno-logical approaches as a basis for development of quantitative instru-ments. Variations of this method can and should be used in bilingual education instructional features studies, but the development of scales should also include verification of generalizability and predictive valid-ity. (Goodrich, 1980: 23–4)

Also of interest is the reference to Carrasco, Guzman, Erickson and Cazden (NIE-G-78-0099) who are exploring ways of quantifying ethnographic infor-mation through videotaping classroom events. Cazden *et al.* (1980) discuss some of these issues in their 'The contribution of ethnographic research to *bicultural* bilingual education'. The point made in these studies is that the culture of the classroom, monolingual or bilingual, must initially be approached through ethnographic procedures for the simple reason that the significance of events, e.g. a boy erasing a blackboard, must emerge emi-cally from the context. The boy may erase the blackboard as punishment or as a favor for his teacher or because he was the last person to write on the board. Until the researcher *understands* this action from its context, the event cannot even be counted as data as the category would be unclear. I find this argument totally convincing.

The boy-at-the-blackboard example comes from NIE 'Planning Paper 6: Issues in applying ethnography to bilingual classroom settings' by Rudes, Goldsamt & Cervenka (1980), which is for our purposes the most explicit of the NIE documents. 'This report is intended to be a conceptual and metho-dological resource for those designing bilingual education research to take place in classroom settings, and a synthesis of the state-of-the-art in that field' (Rudes, Goldsamt & Cervenka, 1980: 2). It is impossible to summarize the 95-page document here, which to a large extent deals with technical

issues of data collection, technical aids equipment like videotaping, protocols, coding frameworks, etc. all within an ethnographic approach to research. There is considerable concern, at the technical level, with avoiding
some of the 'sloppiness' of ethnography and with increasing rater/observer
reliability. There is concern for quantification as well.

The authors reaffirm that qualitative–quantitative studies are not
either–or arrangements and that both types stand to profit from each other.
Quantitative studies gain from 'rich descriptions' and qualitative studies can
benefit from quantitative concerns for reliability and validity. They cite
Esteban Arvizu on a project in Sacramento which is currently using qualitative and quantitative methods to study symbolic interaction:

> Three interrelated (and perhaps concentric) contexts, the community,
> school and bilingual program are being studied by using a series of
> qualitative approaches which each supply information on different
> facets of the context. The same is true of the quantitative techniques
> being used, which supply data on factual, attitudinal, and statistical
> variables. Three levels of the study exist, with the first, and the basis
> for the other two levels, being descriptive ethnography which lasts one
> year. (Rudes, Goldsamt & Cervenka, 1980: 46)

See also Table 6.2.

Rudes, Goldsamt & Cervenka conclude with discussing the joint appli-
cation of ethnographic and quantitative approaches. First, ethnographic
study can serve as a prelude to quantitative study in which variables and
hypothesis are first identified in the former and then 'more rigorously' tested
through the latter approach. Second, the two methods can be used concurrently in the same study, with a methodological separation of the two
approaches. Here they see the quantitative method as the tool of ethnography. Third, ethnographic and quantitative methods may be merged and
used concurrently in investigating the same research questions. This latter
approach they hold likely to be unproductive for reasons 'that the two
methods basically have paradigms which are antagonistic to each other'
(Rudes, Goldsamt & Cervenka, 1980: 70). This reasoning is far from clear
to me, especially as I do not believe the dichotomy to be at the paradigmatic
level. I find it likely that such a position is representative of our ignorance of
such approaches rather than of any inherent impossibility. The next decade
is likely to see considerable advance in research techniques exactly in this
approach of a concurrent merging of qualitative and quantitative methods.
They conclude, 'it should not be forgotten that both methodologies have a
firm place in the study of behavior and interaction in bilingual education settings' (Rudes, Goldsamt & Cervenka, 1980: 73). I could not agree more.

TABLE 6.2   *Framework for research (symbolic interaction)*

Ethnographic study		
Study of community	*Study of school*	*Study of bilingual program*

Methods	
Qualitative	*Quantitative*
1. Participant observation	1. Census
2. Event analysis	2. Survey questionnaires
3. Life history	3. Archival and document search
4. Comparative interviewing	4. Content and frequency analysis of records
5. Ethnographic filming	5. Economic, employment political trend analysis
6. Micro-ethnographic	
7. Projective techniques	

Level 1 — Descriptive ethnography   (first 12 months)
Level 2 — Trend analysis   (second 12 months)
Level 3 — Theory building and hypothesis testing (follow-up to study)

Source: Arvizu, 1980

Notes

1. I do not believe myself that research methodology is of the same category as theoretical paradigms, and hence find the methodological controversy not to be paradigmatic. But that need not worry us here.
2. Marxism has never gained the legitimate academic status in America as it has in Europe, and American social scientists tend to prefer the term group conflict theory in lieu of neo-marxism.

3. For some of the difficulties in measuring other aspects of language proficiency, such as pronunciation, fluent and appropriate speaking, see Canale & Swain (1980). See also Swain (1978), 'School reform through bilingual education: Problems and some solutions in evaluating programs'.

References

BARTH, F. 1969, *Ethnic Groups and Boundaries*. Boston, Mass.: Little, Brown & Co.
BERLINER, D. C. and TIKUNOFF, W. J. 1976, The California beginning teacher evaluation studies: overview of the ethnographic study. *Journal of Teacher Education* 27, 1, 27–34.
BOWLES, S., GINTIS, H. and MEYER, P. 1976, Education, IQ, and the legitimation of the social division of labor. *Berkeley Journal of Sociology* 20, 233–64.
CAMBELL, D. T. and STANLEY, J. C. 1963, *Experimental and Quasi-experimental Designs for Research*. Chicago, Ill.: Rand-McNally.
CANALE, M. and SWAIN, M. 1980, Theoretical bases of communicative approaches to second language teaching and testing. *Applied Linguistics* 1, 1, 1–47.
CAZDEN, C., CARRASCO, R., MALDONADO-GUZMAN, A. A. and ERICKSON, F. 1980. The contribution of ethnographic research to *bicultural* bilingual education. *Current Issues in Bilingual Education*. Washington, DC: Georgetown University.
COOK, T. D. and REICHARDT, C. S. 1979, *Qualitative and Quantitative Methods in Evaluation Research*. Beverly Hills, CA: Sage Publications.
EKSTRAND, L. H. 1980, Vad menas med aktiv tvåspråkighet? *Invandrare och Minoriteter* 2, 14–21.
FILSTEAD, W. J. 1970, *Qualitative Methodology*. Chicago, Ill.: Markham.
—— 1979, Qualitative and quantitative methods in evaluation research. In T. D. COOK and C. S. REICHARDT *Qualitative and Quantitative Methods in Evaluation Research*. Beverly Hills, CA: Sage Publications.
GOODRICH, R. L. 1980, Planning Paper 3: Planning factors for studies of bilingual instructional features. Prepared for the National Institute of Education by Apt Associates, Inc., Cambridge, Mass.
HANSON, G. 1980, Modersmålsklasser och Övergångs modeller. *Invandrare och Minoriteter* 3, 6–8.
KUHN, T. S. 1971, *The Structure of Scientific Revolutions*. Chicago, Ill.: University of Chicago Press.
NIE (National Institute of Education) 1980a, Amendment of solicitation No. NIE-R-80-0025. Washington, DC.
—— 1980b, A compendium of bilingual education and related projects. Washington, DC.
PAULSTON, C. B. 1980, *Bilingual Education: Theories and Issues*. Rowley, Mass.: Newbury House.
PAULSTON, R. G. 1976, *Conflicting Theories of Social and Educational Change*. Pittsburgh, PA: University Center for International Center.
—— 1979, Multiple approaches to the evaluation of educational reform: from cost-benefit to power-benefit analysis. Paper prepared for the International Institute of Educational Planning Seminar on the Organization of Educational Reform at the Local Level, Paris.

RIST, R. C. 1977, On the relations among educational research paradigms: from disdain to detente. *Anthropology and Education Quarterly* 8, 2, 42–9.

—— 1980, Blitzkrieg ethnography: on the transformation of a method into a movement. *Educational Researcher* 9, 2, 9–10.

RUDES, B. A., GOLDSAMT, M. R. and CERVENKA, E. J. 1980, Planning Paper 6: Issues in applying ethnography to bilingual classroom settings. Prepared for the National Institute of Education by Development Associates, Inc., Arlington, VA.

SKUTNABB-KANGAS, T. 1980, Forskare som tyckare. *Invandrare och minoriteter* 3, 9–12.

SWAIN, M. 1978, School reform through bilingual education: problems and some solutions in evaluating programs. *Comparative Education Review* 22, 3, 420–33.

7 Problems in the Comparative Analysis of Bilingual Education

Virtually all the research on bilingual education (BE) is comparative in nature, yet we have not really paid any attention to the problems which a comparative approach entails. The only reference in the literature on bilingual and migrant education which I have come across which specifically mentions some of the problems of a comparative analysis is Ekstrand's (1978: 30) 'Migrant adaptation: A cross-cultural problem' and then only in passing. In this paper I would like to explore some of the functions and problems of a comparative study of bilingual education in order to clarify the question of generalizability of BE research.

As Simon (1969: 63) points out '(m)ost empirical research in psychology, sociology, marketing research, education, anthropology, political science, and all other branches of social science except economics is comparison research, although sometimes the comparison is part of research intended to establish cause and effect'. Comparative study takes different forms in the various disciplines, basically because of the different problem formulations. One claim is that the term 'comparative approach does not, as has sometimes been claimed, properly designate a specific method in social research, but rather a special focus on cross-societal, institutional, or macro-societal aspects of societies and social analysis' (Shils, in Eisenstadt, 1969: 423). The methodological problems then are not distinct from those of any other type of sociological research except as the choice of topic in comparative study may necessitate special types of data.

In sociology, comparative research usually deals with hypothesis testing about social behavior and institutions, through statistical techniques, over a wide sample of societies in order to find universal trends and general laws. Social anthropologists (in which field the term 'comparative method' first seems to have become established) similarly work for 'the development of general propositions about culturally regulated human behavior' which

145

some believe will lead to the discovery of true sociological 'laws', similar to the law of gravity. Leach (1969: 339) points out that this analogy with the natural sciences simply does not work in the study of man because in contradistinction to the subject matter of natural science, man has a will of his own. Instead of discovering laws, the purpose of cross-cultural comparison in social anthropology should be

> to discover what is humanly feasible rather than to demonstrate what is statistically probable. Cross-cultural comparison here becomes a means of understanding the humanity of human beings. It is not a question of demonstrating that culture is like nature, but of showing how culture differs from nature. (Leach, 1969: 341, 342)

In psychology,[1] comparison research need not be cross-cultural but consists of what research is commonly held to be: experimental design and hypothesis testing with pre-specified variables through the collection of quantificational data from groups which are then compared. The problems of comparison here are common to all social and behavioral research but when this type of research design attempts to elucidate questions of bilingual education, there are problems associated with the specific types of data. For example, the crucial necessity to control for SES in studies on BE programs is (or should be) common to all research, but Cummins' (1982) attempt of theory building of L1 and L2 acquisition and their interdependence necessitates the distinction in the language data between CALP (cognitive-academic language proficiency) and BICS (basic interpersonal communicative skills), a problem of conceptualization and operationalization of data specific to this problem formulation. Bilingual education, certainly not a discipline of its own, draws primarily on psychology, anthropology, and sociology in its research and so will share the functions and problems of research in those fields. Science does not solve problems, but it can help people make better *decisions*. That I and so many other people have stopped smoking is certainly the direct result of the findings of medical research, to take an example which involves individual decision making. In bilingual education, the research is typically marked by a practical and empirical approach, often specifically designed to help people make better decisions, such as Löfgren's (1981) *Modersmålsklasser eller sammansatta klasser för barn till invandrare* ('Mother tongue classes or integrated classes for children of immigrants: a theoretical discussion and empirical testing of some selected propositions and development of a casual model for immigrant children's success in school', my translation) or Wrede's (1979) *Elevers', föräldrars och lärares upplevelse och uppfattning av arbetet i tre finska lågstadieklasser i Eskilstuna kommun* ('Students', parents' and teachers' experience and opinion of the work in three Finnish elementary classes in Eskilstuna township', my translation). The problem is, of course, that the decisions they advocate are diametrically opposed, and I think it is exactly the frequent phenomenon of contradictory data in the research of BE which has led to the necessity of a cross-societal, cross-national, cross-cultural approach in order to find universal trends and test hypotheses for the schooling of children in another language than their mother tongue. I have in mind such studies as Ekstrand's (1978) 'Migrant adaptation: A cross-cultural problem' or my own 'Ethnic relations and bilingual education: Accounting for contradictory data' (Paulston, 1975).

Much BE research is evaluation research of specific programs and so by necessity treats the program as the independent variable, but I think most of us are by now in agreement that such findings hold only limited generalizability and that to understand such findings one has to consider school programs or treatments as intervening or contextual variables and look to socio-economic and cultural factors for causal explanations of language acquisition, of school grades, of social mobility, of employment rates, of however one chooses to operationalize program success. One of the major tasks, then, in the comparative study of BE becomes to identify *under what conditions,* the classical question of sociology, children will successfully manage schooling in two languages. This approach typically consists of an analysis of case studies (the evaluation/measurement case studies are not only useful here but indispensable) in light of some guiding hypotheses.

At times the theories which form the bases for studies are also examined in a comparison of the case studies which serve to document the theories: such a study is Ekstrand's (1979) 'Early bilingualism: Theories and facts' where his findings support Cummins' that older students make more efficient language learners. Cummins' (1982) study is interesting in that he deliberately compares two groups of students with different background characteristics, namely upper-middle-class Japanese and Vietnamese refugee students in order to test the generalizability of his interdependence hypothesis. Such studies are rare. Case studies are of course also used to develop typologies of various kinds (see Mackey, 1970). There is also replication of case studies, such as the Culver City replication (Campbell, 1972) of the St Lambert study (Lambert & Tucker, 1972).

Frequent variables in the experimental design type research are sex, age, ethnic identity, sense of self, vocational choice, school grades and high school attendance to mention some I culled from the Swedish research, where the behavior of migrant students is compared with those of Swedish youth. Löfgren and Ouvinen-Birgerstam (1980: 102) make the interesting observation that this research, i.e. research on migrants, 'has to a high degree been characterized by fault-finding, i.e. it has been geared to look for deficiencies' and go on to question the result of such research on migrants' pride and Swedes' attitudes.

I believe these types of research: the search for social conditions which are predictable, theory testing, typology building, replication and the studies with experimental design (which are inherently comparative) constitute the major functions of comparison in BE. In addition, we have contrastive analysis in linguistics and occasionally what amounts to a contrastive analysis even if not so labeled in anthropology, such as Freudenthal, Narrowe & Sachs (n.d.) *Turkar i svensk förort* ('Turks in Swedish suburbia'), where it is specifically the Turks' unSwedish behavior which is singled out for description, also a form of comparison.

Eisenstadt points out that the construction of types for purposes of comparative analysis poses several methodological questions. One of these is the selection of units comparison. Ekstrand (1981) rejects the notion of a critical period in language acquisition while Scovel (1981) breaks down language into separate skills and so argues for a critical period for the acquisition of pronunciation. Their units of comparison are different. I have already mentioned that Cummins (1982) sees it necessary to break down language acquisition into two units he calls CALP and BICS or lately 'context-reduced' and 'context-embedded' language proficiency where the very labels for the units contain a conceptual explanation. Context-reduced language acquisition favors older learners and so sheds further light on the critical period problem.

We talk glibly about immigrants and immigrant education, but who are they? This has caused considerable definitional difficulty for the Swedish statisticians (see Reinans, 1980). We know that the Finns as a group have the lowest percentage of students continuing their schooling after graduation from the compulsory *grundskolan* but who are the Finns? Are the Tornedalfinns Finns? Are the Swedefinns Finns? The answer may seem perfectly obvious but if the question is asked in order to extend the rights to mother tongue instruction the answer is not obvious. The rationale for selection of unit of comparison and analysis lies as always with the research question, with the purpose of the research.

Another problem is the construction of indices through which the variables can be compared. We talk about multicultural education, but what is it? I don't believe that I have ever seen a multicultural education classroom, not even in my own classroom in Tangier where we represented eight different cultures,[2] but until we have a generally accepted construction of indices of what constitutes multilingual education I really can't tell because

I have no way of comparing that classroom with, say, my Katrineholm class-room along the variables of culture.

Comparability of variables is a problem in most research but especially in research which uses case studies for secondary data. Comparing, as is so often done, the Canadian immersion programs with the monolingual school-ing in the L2 of migrant children is a classic error of comparison, of com-paring the noncomparable. The Canadian programs show us, in Leach's terms, what is humanly feasible, but it remains to spell out under what con-ditions. Comparison research often compares against a known standard, be it IQ scores, TOEFL scores or standardized subject matter tests. Much of the Swedish research on migrants compares the scores for immigrant youth (employment figures, gymnasium attendance, and test scores) with the Fin-nish or Swedish national norms. But immigrant youth, as both Ekstrand (1981) and Tingbjörn & Andersson (1981) point out, are primarily members of the working class while the scores are normed on the entire population so that such comparison will give a skewed result. Sometimes faulty compari-son is a result of conceptual confusion, such as comparing foreign language learning with second language learning, sometimes it is just a lack of facts such as comparing a Swedish grade 9 with a US grade 9 in matters of age (Swedes begin school at age 7). I know of no formula for achieving compar-ability except constant vigilance of carefulness and thoughtfulness.

Comparability is closely tied to the problem of sampling. In her review of the literature on IQ and bilingualism, Darcy (1963) found a negative cor-relation in many studies. What she does not point out is the faulty sampling procedures of those studies: most of the subjects were recent immigrants, members of the working class, and apparently in many cases not proficient in English. In cross-national studies, sampling often involves a compromise between representativeness of group or country and equivalence across countries. Osgood, May & Miron (1975) give the example of Indian college students being more highly selected (less representative) than an equivalent sample of Dutch college students. In the Lambert & Klineberg study *Chil-dren's Views of Foreign People: A Cross-national Study* (1967), they wanted to compare children's images of themselves and foreigners as a function of their nationality and age:

> Therefore they wanted both equivalence, in the sense of age levels, sex ratios, intelligence and the like, and representativeness, in the sense of socio-economic level and the like so that differences could not be attri-buted to education of parents, for example. This required a com-promise which in their case appeared as a form of stratified sampling within otherwise equivalent groups. (Osgood, May & Miron, 1975: 20)

Osgood's point is the nature of the compromise depends on the purpose of the research.

Measurement presents a number of problems. One is at the heart of all research, that of finding empirical proxies to measure for conceptual variables, the problem of operationalization. I have argued elsewhere (Paulston, 1980) for the need to evaluate the BE programs with indicators like school drop out rates and employment figures in addition to standardized test scores and won't repeat that argument here. Basically that is a problem in goal perception. Mostly in comparison research, I should think, the operationalization problem is one of validity of the instruments. In many of the Darcy studies, the IQ tests really functioned as language proficiency tests and it was not IQ one compared but knowledge of English. Working with case studies, one needs to pay attention to the instruments used. Time of treatment fits in marginally here. I remember one dissertation which attempted to evaluate a bilingual education program after eight hours of treatment. That is just plain silly. The Rock Point study (Rosier & Holm, 1980) needed six years to show a positive result.

Sometimes the problem of operationalization has to do with finding indicators for concepts which are unique to research on bilingualism. The rationale most often cited for the Swedish policies on mother tongue teaching is that of *halvspråkighet,* semilingualism or more correctly double semilingualism, a notion popularized by Hansegård in 1968 which claims that bilingual children may learn neither of their two languages well. The press abounds with reference to semilingualism, the Finnish associations claim it as a rationale in their demand for a monolingual Finnish university in Sweden, and university students essays repeatedly make comments that 'researchers are agreed that semilingualism . . .' The fact of the matter is that semilingualism as a conceptual variable has never been operationalized to anyone's satisfaction so researchers cannot very well agree on something that may not exist. Actually, they don't agree: Loman's (1974) work is noticeable in this context. The counter argument leads into the quantitative/ qualitative data discussion. Finding an empirical proxy for semilingualism will trivialize the concept, goes the claim. If it is a linguistic phenomenon, it ought to be observable, say the linguists. (See e.g. Hyltenstam & Stroud, 1982.) At present, there is a stand still. But as a major problem in Swedish research, operationlization of *halvspråkighet* remains. Before it becomes the major rationale for Swedish language policies, the existence of such a language phenomenon needs to be established, measured and described or the notion should be dismissed.

Qualitative data has other problems in comparison research. Cross-cultural anthropologists worry a lot about the generalizability of their data, mostly for reasons of validity. Would another anthropologist with other training and maybe another worldview have seen and described the same things, reached the same interpretations? In the immigrant research one will occasionally find statements, comments, poems by the immigrants themselves which is a form of operationalizing attitudes and feelings. When such statements are representative (i.e. reliable) of the group, they make excellent data, but they are of course especially vulnerable to researcher bias in their selection. I don't, for instance, expect to see Richard Rodriguez (1982), who writes movingly and beautifully about his upbringing and goes on record against bilingual education, cited in Chicano research.

Another measurement problem is that of testing. There exists an entire literature on minority testing and I won't go into it here except to mention three issues in passing. First of all, there is the meaning of testing which may vary from culture to culture. Cole *et al.* (1971) have documented this in detail in their work with Kpelles. Donald Erickson, who tested the Navajo children in the Rough Rock study (Erickson *et al.*, 1969), wrote me in answer to a question about the testing:

> In observing the students while they responded to the achievement tests, I was convinced that in many cases we were getting measurements of attitudes regarding time, competition, the importance of tests, etc., much more than we were getting data on what the tests purported to tap. The typical achievement test, I fear is a rather stupid way of testing many American Indian students. (Private correspondence, June 26, 1973)

This practical-technical objection is echoed in the conflict perspective oriented attack by Edelsky *et al.* on Swain & Cummins (1979) for, of all things, propagating a language deficit theory:

> When some people interpret a test question as a hostile demand for disclosure, while others interpret that same test question as a harmless demand for a performance, then it is inaccurate to claim that the two groups experienced the same standardized situation and task. The overall consequence of reliance on data from such measures and settings is to make 'the hegemony of the successful look legitimate because of their superior performance on school tests'. (Edelsky *et al.*, 1983)

Edelsky *et al.*'s major objection to Swain & Cummins is that they don't like standardized test scores and measurement research, i.e. they deny the validity of such operationalization. The neo-marxist interpretation apart, testing does remain a problem in cross-cultural research.

There is also the problem of translation and standardization of testing instruments. Osgood, May & Miron (1975: 15 ff.) discuss the problems of translation, basically a question of choosing exact equivalent or culturally corresponding items, i.e. Christian Sunday corresponds with Muslim Friday. They go on to point out that since the purpose of standardization is to render data from diverse samples comparable, this may well mean in cross-cultural research the deliberate choice of different instructions and even procedures. Trial and error with native informants and careful pretesting is an obvious strategy.

So far the discussion has concerned methodological problems. But as Eisenstadt points out, the construction of problems for comparative analysis also engenders theoretical and analytical problems. Types constructed out of variables imply some assumption about the importance of such variables, such as for example Cummins' CALP and BICS.

> Such analytical problems tend to become even more important in attempts to 'explain' varied types of institutions, organizations, or pattern of behavior in terms of some broader conditions. In most comparative analysis such explanation aims . . . to elucidate the conditions under which such varied societal types emerge and continue to exist and function . . . (Eisenstadt, 1969: 425)

Let me illustrate. In order to understand the behavior of immigrants, including their language behavior, we have used the constructs of ethnicity, ethnic groups and ethnic boundaries (Barth, 1969; Schermerhorn, 1970). But it may well be that ethnicity is not the best choice of construct to explain the situation of the Finns in Sweden compared with that of the other immigrants. I am at this point tentatively considering the situation of the Finns as an extension of geographic nationalism rather than one of ethnic boundary maintenance, a construct that serves well for the Turks and the Assyrians. The choice between nationalism and ethnicity then is an analytical problem and arguing that out will constitute the topic for a future paper, but briefly, that construct with its covariation of variables which most simply can account for the most data is usually considered the better choice. To the degree such a choice will carry explanatory power, it becomes a theoretical problem.

Finally, I must mention the kind of problems that come under the heading of ethical problems in comparative research. They have been extensively discussed in the literature (see e.g. Brislin, Bochner & Lanner, 1975) and I mostly want just to acknowledge their existence. TESOL has adopted a set of ethical guidelines for research in English as a Second Language and I think all academics should discuss these matters with their students. The fault-finding type of research that Löfgren & Ouvinen-Birgerstam mention is an ethical problem. Research on immigrants easily enough becomes a form of internal colonization, and that is also an ethical problem. Most of all maybe, what do the immigrants get out of all this research, not in vague terms of future policies but right now? It is a glib and frequent question but difficult to answer.

Sound generalization and prediction depend ultimately on good judgment, which in turn depends on 'an *understanding* of the various forces which underlie the process. Gaining such an understanding is more a matter of saturation in the situation than of scientific technique' (Simon, 1969: 357). My hope is that this discussion will help contribute to our good judgment in understanding the problems in the comparative analysis of BE so that we safely and accurately generalize from the appropriate data.

Notes

1. Comparative psychology proper is concerned with the behavior of different species of living organisms, typically animals, and leads to the specification of similarities and differences in behavior between species in order to relate an animal's behavior to its evolutionary background. (Waters & Bunnel, 1969.)
   'Cross-cultural psychology is a meta-method with all of the areas of psychology grist to its mill' (Brislin, Bochner & Lonner, 1975: 7).
2. Arab, Berber, English, Gibraltarian, Indian, Spanish, Swedish, US.

References

BARTH, F. 1969, *Ethnic Groups and Boundaries*. Oslo: Universitets förlaget.

BRISLIN, R. W., BOCHNER, S. and LONNER, W. J. 1975, *Cross-cultural Perspectives on Learning*. New York: Wiley.

CAMPBELL, R. 1972, Bilingual education in Culver City. Workpapers: Teaching English as a Second Language, 6, 87–92. Los Angeles: University of California.

COLE, M., GAY, J., GLICK, J. and SHARP, D. 1971, *The Cultural Context of Learning and Thinking*. New York: Basic Books.

CUMMINS, J. 1982, Linguistic interdependence among Japanese and Vietnamese immigrant students. In C. RIVERA (ed.) *The Measurement of Communicative Proficiency: Models and Applications*. Washington, DC: Center for Applied Linguistics.

DARCY, N. 1963, A review of the literature on the effects of bilingualism upon the measurement of intelligence. *J. Genetic Psychology* 103, 259–82.

EDELSKY, C., HUDELSON, S., FLORES, B., BARKIN, F., ALTWERGER, B. and GILBERT, K. 1983, CALP, BICS, and semilingualism: a language deficit theory for the 80's. *Applied Linguistics* 4.

EISENSTADT, S. 1969, Social institutions: comparative study. *International Encyclopedia of the Social Sciences*. New York: Macmillan.

EKSTRAND, L. H. 1978, Migrant adaptation: a cross-cultural problem. In R. FREUDENSTEIN (ed.) *Teaching the Children of Immigrants*. Brussels: Didier.
—— 1979, Early bilingualism: theories and facts. *Reprints and Miniprints*. Malmö: School of Education.
—— 1981, Språk, Identitet, Kultur. *Reprints and Miniprints* 391. Malmö: School of Education.

ERICKSON, D. *et al.* 1969, Community school at Rough Rock — an evaluation of the office of economic opportunity. Springfield, Va.: Department of Economic Opportunity.

FREUDENTHAL, S., NARROWE, J. and SACHS, L. n.d., *Turkar i svensk förort*. Socialantropologiska Institutionen, Stockholm University.

HANSEGÅRD, N. E. 1968, *Tvåspråkighet eller halvspråkighet?* Stockholm: Aldus/Bonniers.

HYLTENSTAM, K. and STROUD, C. 1982, Halvspråkighet-ett förbrukat slagord. *Invandrare och Minoriteter* 3.

LAMBERT, W. and KLINEBERG, O. 1967, *Children's Views of Foreign Peoples: A Cross-national Study*. New York: Appleton-Century-Croft.

LAMBERT, W. and TUCKER, R. 1972, *Bilingual Education of Children: The St. Lambert Experiment*. Rowley, Mass.: Newbury House.

LEACH, E. R. 1969, The comparative method in anthropology. *International Encyclopedia of the Social Sciences*. New York: Macmillan.

LÖFGREN, H. 1981, Modersmålsklasser eller sammansatta klasser för barn till invandrare. Pedagogiska Institutionen, Lund University.

LÖFGREN, H. and OUVINEN-BIRGERSTAM, P. 1980, Försök med en tvåspråkig model för undervisning av invandrarbarn. Pedagogiska Institutionen, Lund University.

LOMAN, B. 1974, Till frågan om tvåspråkighet och halvspråkighet. *Språk och Samhälle*. Lund: Gleerup.

MACKEY, W. 1970, A typology of bilingual education. *Foreign Language Annals* 3, 596–608.

OSGOOD, C. E., MAY, W. H. and MIRON, M. S. 1975, *Cross-cultural Universals of Affective Meaning*. Urbana, Ill.: University of Illinois Press.

PAULSTON, C. B. 1975, Ethnic relations and bilingual education: accounting for contradictory data. In R. C. TROIKE and N. MODIANO (eds) *Proceedings of the First Inter-American Conference on Bilingual Education*. Washington, DC: Center for Applied Linguistics.
—— 1980, *Bilingual Education: Theories and Issues*. Rowley, Mass.: Newbury House.

REINANS, S. 1980, Vilka är invandrarna. Manuscript. EIFO, Stockholm.

RODRIGUEZ, R. 1982, *Hunger of Memory: The Education of Richard Rodriguez*. Boston: Godine.

ROSIER, P. and HOLM, W. 1980, *The Rock Point Experience: A Longitudinal Study of a Navajo School Program*. Washington, DC: Center for Applied Linguistics.

SCHERMERHORN, R. H. 1970, *Comparative Ethnic Relations: A Framework for Theory and Research*. New York: Random House.

SCOVEL, T. 1981, The effects of neurological age on nonprimary language acquisition. In R. ANDERSON (ed.) *New Dimensions in Research on the Acquisition and Use of a Second Language*. Rowley, Mass.: Newbury House.

PROBLEMS IN COMPARATIVE ANALYSIS   155

SIMON, J. L. 1969, *Basic Research Methods in Social Science: The Art of Empirical Investigation*. New York: Random House.
SWAIN, M. and CUMMINS, J. 1979, Bilingualism, cognitive functioning, and education. *Language Teaching and Linguistics: Abstracts* 4–18.
TINGBJÖRN, G. and ANDERSSON, A. B. 1981, *Invandrarbarnen och tvåspråkigheten*. Stockholm: Liber.
WATERS, R. H. and BUNNELL, B. N. 1969, Comparative psychology. *International Encyclopedia of the Social Sciences*. New York: Macmillan.
WREDE, G. 1979, *Elevers, föräldrars och lärares upplevelse och uppfattning av arbetet i tre finska lågstadieklasser i Eskilstuna Kommun*. Pedagogiska Institutionen, University of Uppsala.

8 Language Planning

Most scholars have agreed to limit the term language planning to 'the organized pursuit of solutions to language problems, typically at the national level' (Fishman, 1973: 23–4). The degree of 'organized' varies; a language planning process that shares Jernudd's specifications of the orderly and systematic (a) establishment of goals, (b) selection of means, and (c) prediction of outcomes is an exception rather than the rule (Jernudd, 1973: 11–23). Heath's study of language policy in Mexico (Heath, 1972) illustrates how language decisions are made during the history of a nation: decisions are primarily made on political and economic grounds and reflect the values of those in political power. Linguistic issues *per se* are of minor concern. Since the matters discussed are always overtly those of language, there is considerable confusion about the salient issues debated in language planning, whether they are, in fact, matters of political, economic, religious, sociocultural or linguistic concerns.

In discussing language problems, then, it is important for their identification, analysis and treatment to understand whether they are legitimately problems of language or whether the language situation is merely symptomatic of social and cultural problems. To this end I find it useful to distinguish between language cultivation and language policy, where *language cultivation* deals with matters of language and *language policy* with matters of society and nation.[1] Jernudd (1973) has suggested the terms 'language determination', 'language development' and 'language implementation', where determination roughly corresponds to policy and development to cultivation; he also points out that there exists a relationship between the two. I would like to take this one step further and suggest that determination, development and implementation are sub-sets of cultivation as well as of policy so that a simple table looks like Table 8.1. Here *determination* refers to the initial decision(s) among alternate goals, means and outcomes, although means may not form part of determination. Official language choice and commitment to bilingual education like the US Title VII Bilingual Education Act are typical examples. *Development* refers to the working out of means and strategies (Rubin's terms) to achieve one's putative outcomes (Rubin, 1973); the urgent preparation of texts for bilingual education in countries like Peru is a crucial step in order to be able to implement the policy of the Plan Nacional de Educación Bilingue. The preparation of vocabulary lists, normative grammars and spelling manuals are other examples. And teacher training deserves to be mentioned here, when national educational policy is being developed.

TABLE 8.1

Language cultivation	Language policy
Determination Development Implementation	Determination Development Implementation

Determination without development is not likely to bring about implementation. The mere statement that Swahili is the official language of Kenya is not likely to decrease the use of English (German, 1973: 77). Development then becomes negative, discouraging or stigmatizing certain language behaviors on an institutional level. The standardized reading tests in the United States, which systematically discriminate against good black readers, is another example of the negative results which occur where there has been inadequate development of a national decision — that is, to teach everyone to read.

Implementation finally is the actual attempt to bring about the desired goals (Jernudd, 1973). The sale of grammars and dictionaries, the distribution of textbooks, the language used in the mass media, and the Cuban Literacy Campaign in 1961 are all implementations of previous determination and development.

Occasionally the chronological order of determination, development and implementation may seem to be reversed so that the determination simply becomes the official ratification of already implemented or accepted language use, as when the French Academy legalized masculine gender for *auto* long after it was common practice to say *un auto*. On closer thought, however, the number of Frenchmen saying *un auto* should not be thought of as the implementation of the academy's decision, but rather as a crucial input on that decision. Some of the factors least discussed in the literature on language planning are the factors which serve to influence the decisions in the determination stage. Rioting hordes in India, the folk high schools in Norway and a large Navajo-speaking population in the United States have all had their input on decisions made about language, even though the influence has been vastly disparate in nature. Existing language use does not form part of the planning process, but is rather a major influence on every facet of that process. In my discussion of language planning I am not dealing with the factors which serve to influence determination, development and implementation, but I have long thought them to be the most important aspects of language planning. There is as yet no theory of language planning that can systematically deal with such inputs.

I have left until last the basic difficulty of determining how a given language problem is classified as belonging to the cultivation or the policy category. In discussing this difficulty, I hope to make three things clear. First, that there is a much more continuing interrelationship between the

TABLE 8.2

Criteria	Cultivation approach	Policy approach
Determination		
1. Who makes the decision?	Language specialists, i.e. linguists, philologists, language teachers, native informants, etc.	Government officials, agencies, ministries, etc.
2. Does decision concern native or other language?	Decision about official native language of policy makers	Decision about choice of official language or about second or foreign language of policy makers
3. Whom does the decision affect?	Decision affects language behavior of elites and policy makers as well	Decision affects only subordinate classes or groups
Development		
4. Factors in evaluating results?	Primarily linguistic or paedo-linguistic	Primarily non-linguistic, such as economic, political, ideological, etc.
Implementation		
5. Factors in evaluating results?	Passive acceptance	Strong attitudes, either negative or positive

two approaches than is normally recognized. Secondly, just as in linguistics, to borrow a metaphor, the same surface structures may have different underlying deep structures. So many observed language phenomena seem to be the same problem, for example, the standardization of *nynorsk* and Hindi as official languages, when in fact very different language planning processes are involved (Haugen, 1966; Das Gupta, 1970). And thirdly, the model will help indicate at what times and in what areas it would be reasonable to expect that the language specialist could actively contribute to the language planning process.

I have attempted to isolate the basic elements which distinguish reported case studies of language planning from one another and to formulate these as criteria by which any event in the planning chain can be assigned to either the cultivation or policy approach. My concern has not been with abstract notions but with the realities of language planning (Rubin & Jernudd, 1971: xxii). The criteria are as in Table 8.2.

Criterion 1: Who Makes the Decision?

This is a relatively clear-cut category. In most cases it is quite clear whether the decision is made by language specialists, such as linguists, philologists, language teachers or native informants, and so belongs to the cultivation approach or is made by government officials of various kinds, such as in agencies or ministeries, and belongs in the policy approach. Like Jernudd (1973), I have limited to language planning such actions which require governmental authorization; others he refers to as instances of language treatment, examples being Australian Broadcasting Corporation pronunciation guidance, newspaper columnist advice and so on. These I would consider as part of the eventual input on the determination and development stages. However, more often proof-readers and columnists turn to the dictionaries and word-lists developed by language specialists, so that the printed consequences of the columnist's advice actually reflects the implementation of previous determination and development. Thus columnist advice which reflects standard and dictionary usage is implementation; columnist advice which goes counter to standard and dictionary usage (for instance, that it is all right to split infinitives in English) becomes input for future determinations.

There are in many countries official governmental academies, like the French Academy and the Swedish Royal Academy, whose members are not primarily language specialists and who make decisions about language. According to this criterion, these decisions would seem to be policy decisions. I clearly consider them under the cultivation approach for these reasons. The primary criterion for membership in this type of academy is the demonstration of the highest order of *Kultur* appropriate within that particular culture, and it is as educated and cultured men that they are asked to form their decisions, not as government officials. Criteria 2 and 3 clarify this fuzzy area.

There is another occurrence when the category looks muddled. It does happen that linguists and language experts go into politics and/or become government officials (Das Gupta, 1972). Ivar Aasen in Norway (Haugen, 1972) and Luis Cabrera in Mexico (Heath, 1972: 93, 121) are examples of this. Their linguistic expertise should then be regarded as input into what are clearly policy decisions. Again, Criteria 2 and 3 will clarify this.

Criterion 2: Is the Decision About the Native or Another Language?

Cultivation decisions are usually about the official and native language of the policy makers, as in the French example of *auto* above. Norms for French Canadian are set by speakers of French Canadian, criteria for developing technological word-lists in Swedish are made by Swedes, and so on. Policy decisions typically concern either second or foreign languages for the policy makers or the choice of an official language. Those responsible for the authorization of the Plan Nacional de Educación Bilingüe in Peru or for the Bilingual Education Act in the United States do not speak Arabela or Navajo.

Two points need clarification. I would consider the development and maintenance of a standard written form of a language as a matter of cultivation, normally undertaken by speakers of that language. However, cultures that today do not possess a written code of their language do not have the technical skill of developing a writing system, and in such situations Criterion 2 will not hold, since decisions about reducing language to writing usually are made by outside linguists, frequently by missionary groups like the Summer Institute of Linguistics. These linguists, on the other hand, do learn the target language, and their development decisions are based upon the language use of native speakers. Note, however, that the initial decision, namely, to develop a writing system for, say, Arabela, very often needs official approval and that is a policy decision.

The other point concerns the nature of dialect and language. *Language standardization*, most frequently a matter of selecting one norm from several regional variations, is a matter of language cultivation; *language choice*, the selection of an official code from two or more codes, is language policy. When the cases are clear, as with standardizing Czech, or choosing Hindi and English as official languages in India, there is no confusion, but consider Norway's *nynorsk* and *riksnorsk*. Normally one would consider two codes spoken within the same country and having identical phonemic systems, virtually identical syntax, most of their vocabulary in common and differing primarily only in morphology, to be dialects of the same language, and so expect that the language planning which has taken place in Norway during this century to be the concern of language cultivation (Haugen, 1966). But each code has its own written grammars and dictionaries, fiction and non-fiction are written in both codes and recognized and accepted as such by the Norwegian people, and most importantly, political parties have espoused the adaptation *in toto* of one code or the other for reasons of nationalism, socialism and other ideological values. It is clearly for non-linguistic reasons that Haugen considers the two codes to be separate languages, and hence it follows that language choice may involve selection of codes which, by purely linguistic criteria, might be considered dialects. It is also clear that a great deal of language cultivation preceded the adaptation of Aasen's *Landsmal* (later called *nynorsk*) as the official language. There is a constant criss-crossing between policy determinations and cultivation determinations: The *Storting* (parliament) authorized the Ministry of Church and Education to appoint a permanent Language Board 'whose goal should be to promote the rapprochement of the two written languages on the basis of Norwegian folk speech . . .' (Haugen, 1972: 138). The board eventually presented the *Storting* with a proposal for a textbook norm which was adopted for use in the schools after two days of full-scale debate. A schematization of the language planning events would look as shown in Figure 8.1, where (1) represents the decision on the need for a textbook norm; (2) the ministry charging the board with preparing a textbook norm; (3) the board deciding on guidelines

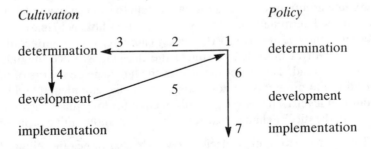

FIGURE 8.1

and policies for the preparation of the textbook norm; (4) the preparation of the textbook norm proposal; (5) the presentation of the proposal to the *Storting*; (6) the adoption of the norm; (7) referral to the ministry for development and implementation.

I commented earlier that this model does not account for the factors influencing the decisions made among the various events in the language-planning process. There is little reason to believe that the board was completely objective in discharging its task; its members were carefully selected equally to represent both languages for a variety of interest groups concerned about language. Although their task (the actual work was done by two linguists) lies in the realm of language cultivation, clearly their decisions were influenced by their ideological orientation.

Criterion 3: Whose Language Behavior Does the Decision Affect?

This is a doubtful category, which may not hold, but the issues raised do need to be considered. Part of the difficulty lies in the vagueness of 'affecting language behavior'. By that I mean 'actual, productive change of present language behavior' if the proposed decision were implemented. If Hindi became the only official language in India, Hindi speakers would presumably not have to learn English. This would represent a change in language behavior, but not a productive one. Spelling reforms affect social elites, policy makers and schoolchildren equally. All language-planning activity which comes under the heading of language cultivation seems to affect both the elites and the policy makers as well as the rest of the population. The elites and the policy makers do not always represent the same groups. This is the case in Norway, and one of the basic difficulties of implementation.

On the other hand, when decisions affect only the language behavior of subordinate groups or classes, these cases seem to be clear examples of language policy determination. The US Congress is not likely to learn Navajo, just because they passed Title VII; literacy campaigns do not affect the language behavior of those who instigate the campaigns, since they already know how to read. This is not to say that the language behaviors of others involved in the programs do not change on the developmental and implementational levels. The language skills needed for bilingual education, for education, drastically change teacher recruitment and training programs.

There are many policy decisions which also affect the elites; from foreign-language requirements in the school curriculum and medium of instruction in the schools to selection of official languages. Especially in the latter case, it is important to realise that governments and elites may have conflicting interests, and that many nations have groups of elites with conflicting interests. Many language policy decisions which result in open strife are owed just to the opposition of competing interest groups within the higher levels of social stratification. Many of the African nations prefer a neutral world language as the official language rather than favoring one of the many native languages, isomorphic with tribal boundaries.

As a final comment on the criteria for analyzing determination decisions as belonging to the cultivation or policy approach, I believe they are listed in order of importance. Criterion 1 overrides the others, and 2 and 3 are useful primarily if 1 does not clearly discriminate between cultivation or policy. If Criteria 2 and 3 conflict, I believe 2 to be more significant.

Criterion 4: Factors in Evaluating the Results on the Development Level

(That is, the produced materials such as dictionaries, word-lists, readers, textbooks and programs, such as curriculum and teacher training.)

This criterion is basically a corollary of Criterion 1: work produced by language specialists is judged by linguistic or paedo-linguistic criteria, and work prepared by government representatives is evaluated by non-linguistic criteria, such as by economic, political, ideological and other factors.

Two points need consideration. From an examination of case studies, it seems evident that, in every decision about language, if it is to stand any chance of implementation and achieving planned goals, such determination must at one stage be developed by language specialists. Political ideology is not sufficient for standardizing languages or eliminating distasteful loan words. An exception are policies which prohibit or stigmatize the use of specified languages, such as the earlier prohibition of Quechua in the Peruvian army and of Spanish in American schools. Such policies are often tacitly understood rather than officially ratified, a problematic concern in historical research (Heath, 1973). But any determination decision about official languages, language development, bilingual education and the like, which is firmly intended to become implemented necessitates a cultivation-development stage. Indeed, it seems probable that one can judge the seriousness of intent of the determination by whether a schematization of the language planning process includes a cultivation-development stage.

In many nations, language specialists needed for cultivation-development are incorporated into official or government agencies, such as in the Bureau of Indian Affairs in the US in the 1930s, the Ministry of Education in Peru and the Academy of the Hebrew Language in Israel. But they work there by virtue of and in the capacity of being language specialists, and the nature of their work is that of language cultivation. Often they work under the supervision and jurisdiction of government officials who do not possess their specifically needed skills — a potential conflict situation (Das Gupta, 1972, 157–65).

And this is the second point. Work produced by language specialists should be evaluated by linguistic and paedo-linguistic criteria, but often this is not the case, and I find it imperative in analyzing language-planning processes that one be very clear about which set of criteria is being applied in discussing developmental products.

To discuss in Kenya in linguistic terms whether English or Swahili better expresses scientific concepts obscures the issue and confuses the argument because the matter is one of emerging nationalism. Such arguments should be considered as input on future policy decisions, not as evaluation of developed products.

Cultivational developments are often judged by both linguistic and non-linguistic criteria. Textbooks are an excellent example, as they serve to socialize children in the cultural and ideological values of the dominant group. A textbook may be excellent by linguistic criteria, but in content go counter to the political or religious ideology of the government (Boggio *et al.*, 1973). This is exactly what happened in Peru, where a new set had to be commissioned to meet the Ministry of Education's non-linguistic criteria. Obviously it is useless and at times confusing to argue such decisions by linguistic criteria.

Economic concerns are also often voiced in the development of textbooks in multilingual situations. Such non-linguistic criteria should be seen as contextual constraints on cultivation-development and of crucial importance in the planning process. Unless constraints are properly understood and accounted for, there is very little likelihood of successful implementation. Fishman (1973: 36) discusses contextual constraints (in the terminology of planning) as unexpected system linkages: '. . . the unexpected system linkages may be indeed of greater moment than the ones of direct interest to the language planner'. This point cannot be stressed sufficiently, especially as the concept of unexpected system linkages is meant to account for planning failures (by professional planners, referred to as 'unexpected outcomes'), and by taking contextual constraints into consideration, one would assure successful implementation. Besides the difficulty of foreseeing the unexpected, I suspect that language planners, that is, language policy makers, may be very aware of these system linkages, but for ideological reasons consider their policy worth the battle. To illustrate, Heath (1972: 143–4) accounts for the failure of bilingual education in Mexico in the 1950s as not the fault of the method but rather 'of the teachers who had ambivalent attitudes about the method or were not adequately trained in the linguistic skills and anthropological assumptions necessary to support the method'. I find these inadequate reasons which do not account for the real problem, which is linkage of race, internal colonization (Cotler, 1968; Paulston, 1970), cholofication (Patch, 1967; Stein, 1972), and *arribismo* (Delgado, 1969: 133–9). Societies will typically blame the schools, the teacher, the method for matters which are symptomatic of social ills and beyond the control of any individuals.

Now, I have myself discussed these concepts, these system linkages, with high officials in the Ministry of Education in Peru (June 1972), and there is no question but that they know and understand the contextual constraints on their bilingual education policy, which are similar to those of Mexico's. They prefer to fail than not to try — and who is to say that they will not succeed. I for one would not want the responsibility of predicting failure on the basis of theoretical notions in the social sciences for a program of which I approve morally.

But to return to the evaluation of cultivation-development. A schematization of the events related to the textbook development within the language-planning process in Peru would be as shown in Figure 8.2, where (1) represents decisions by the Ministry of Education of sweeping reforms in education (Peru, Ley General de Educación, 1972; Escobar, 1972a, 1972b), (2) subsequently the ministry decides on new textbooks, (3) textbooks are commissioned, (4) developed, (5) and returned to those in the ministry in charge of developing new textbooks, where (6) they are rejected, (7) a new set is commissioned, (8) developed, (9) submitted to the ministry, (10) accepted, and (11) implemented.

The points I want to make from this schematization are (a) that language specialists can work effectively and forcefully (no doubt influenced by their ideological values) only when the events in the language-planning process fall under the category of cultivation; (b) that linguistic criteria can be validly and effectively applied only to events in the cultivation category; and (c), when linguistic arguments are applied to advocate or criticize events under policy, they are likely to be colored by the ideological orientation of the language specialist and ineffective unless they are adopted by those involved in determining or implementing policy.

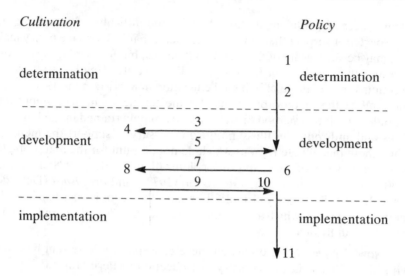

Cultivation   *Policy*

FIGURE 8.2

However, giving advice is very different from advocating a specific policy. When the linguist is asked as consultant to advise (that is, give input to policy decisions), he is very likely to see and suggest options and possible future consequences for each option. A recent anecdote will illustrate this. A Canadian language specialist was asked to evaluate the foreign-language teaching system in an Arab nation in the Middle East. As the medium of instruction at the university level is in English and the students have difficulties with it, he suggested that they consider English instead of Classical Arabic as the medium of instruction during the last two years in high school. The suggestion was promptly rejected for reasons of nationalism and religion, symbolized by Classical Arabic. The government official understood very well the merit of the suggestion for increased efficiency of English teaching, but for him efficiency of English teaching was not the primary function of high school education. It is crucial in evaluating educational language planning that one consider the function of education in that society. The linguist readily accepted the decision; it was not within his domain to question the function of education of that nation. Some time thereafter, however, another government official became minister of education, and he saw the practical merit of the language specialist's recommendations. Consequently, a program, carefully evaluated, is now being carried out, which uses English as the medium of instruction, and which promises to become a model program for similar situations.

Criterion 5: Factors in Evaluating Results of Implementation

The overriding factor in deciding whether an implementation stems from an initial cultivation or policy determination seems to lie in the manner in which it is received by the target population. The implementation of cultivation determinations are normally accepted passively; no one except cantankerous individuals reacted violently to the Swedish spelling reform in 1905. Policy implementations, on the other hand, are typically received with strong attitudes, either negative or positive. The target population may be unanimous or split in its attitudes. The acceptance of Hebrew as a national language was received with strong positive attitudes which enabled its subsequent development and represents a typical language policy. Necessary to this development was later cultivation exemplified in the work of the Hebrew Language Academy whose word-lists, to my knowledge, were never received with public elation (Bar-Adon, 1973).

The very recent interest in language-attitude studies is illustrative of the increasing understanding in the field of language planning of the importance which attitudes play in the successful implementation of language policies. The prediction of attitudes towards alternative language policies is considered an important aspect in theoretical speculations about language planning as a discipline.

To sum up my discussion of language planning, I hope to have demonstrated by the schematizations of case studies of language-planning processes that there is a constant interrelationship between language cultivation and language policy, a relationship usually ignored in the literature on language planning. I hold it important to distinguish between the two approaches as the work of the language specialist belongs in the cultivation category, and much confusion results when linguistic and paedo-linguistic criteria are used to assess language policies. Certainly the language specialist as citizen has both a right and responsibility to voice his concerns about policies, but when he does so, it should be recognized that his interpretation of phenomena may, like any social scientist, be influenced by his personal ideology. The proceedings from the Seminar on Bilingual Education in Lima in January 1972 are more than illustrative of this point (Peru, Ministerio de Educación, 1972).

I also hope to have indicated that another area where the language specialist can contribute is as consultant providing input to policy decisions on all levels. Unfortunately, government officials do not often base language decisions on language data, either out of ignorance or because political considerations are given precedence. Only by taking the initiative in sensitizing decision makers to the importance of linguistic input in language planning can linguists have the kind of impact that is needed.

Note

1. These terms correspond to Heinz Kloss' terms corpus planning and status planning which are more frequently used today in the literature on language planning. 'We can say that "corpus planning" refers to the technical linguistic aspects of language planning while "status planning" refers to policy formulation aimed at enforcing the choice of sociolinguistic and linguistic patterns decided upon' (Daoust-Blais, 1983: 231).

References

BAR-ADON, A. 1973, The rise and decline of an upper-Galillee dialect. In J. RUBIN and R. SHUY (eds) *Language Planning: Current Issues and Research*. Washington, DC: Georgetown University Press.

BOGGIO, A., LORA, C., RIOFRIO, G. and RONCAGLIOLO, R. 1973, *Cuesta ariba o cuesta abajo?: un analysis critico de los textos de lecturnade primaria*. Lima: Centro de Estudios y Promoción de Desarrollo.

COTLER, J. 1968, The mechanics of internal domination and social change in Peru. *Studies in Comparative Development* 3, 12, 67–75.

DAOUST-BLAIS, D. 1983, Corpus and status language planning in Quebec: a look at linguistic education. In J. COBARRUBIAS and J. A. FISHMAN (eds) *Progress in Language Planning*. Berlin: Mouton.

DAS GUPTA, J. 1970, *Language Conflict and National Development: Group Politics and National Language Policy in India*. Berkeley, Calif.: University of California Press.

—— 1972, Language planning and public policy. Analytical outline of the policy process related to language planning in India. In R. SHUY (ed.) *Sociolinguistics: Current Trends and Prospects* (pp. 157–65), report on the Twenty-third Annual Round-Table Meeting. Washington, DC: Georgetown University Press.

DELGADO, C. 1969, An analysis of the 'arribismo' in Peru. *Human Organisation* 28, 2, 133–9.

ESCOBAR, A. 1972a, *Lenguaje y discriminación social en America Latina*. Lima: Milla Batres.

—— (ed.) 1972b, *El reto del multilinguismo en el Peru*. Peru-Problema No. 9. Lima: Instituto de Estudios Peruanos.

FISHMAN, J. A. 1973, Language modernization and planning in comparison with other types of national modernization and planning. *Language in Society* 2, 1, 23–42.

GORMAN, T. 1973, Language allocation and language planning. In J. RUBIN and R. SHUY (eds) *Language Planning: Current Issues and Research*. Washington, DC: Georgetown University Press.

HAUGEN, E. 1966, *Language Conflict and Language Planning: The Case of Modern Norwegian*. Cambridge, Mass.: Harvard University Press.

—— 1972, *The Ecology of Language*. Stanford, Calif.: Stanford University Press.

HEATH, S. B. 1972, *Telling Tongues: Language Policy in Mexico — Colony to Nation*. New York: Teachers College Press.
—— 1973, Language status achievement: policy-approaches to the United States. Colonial and early national perspectives. Report to the research seminar in bilingual education, TESOL Convention, San Juan.
JERNUDD, B. 1973, Language planning as a type of language treatment. In J. RUBIN and R. SHUY (eds) *Language Planning: Current Issues and Research* (pp. 11–23). Washington, DC: Georgetown University Press.
PATCH, R. W. 1967, La Prada, Lima's market. Serrano and Criollo, the confusion of race with class. AUFSR, West Coast South America Series, 14, 2, 3–9.
PAULSTON, R. G. 1970, Estratificatión social, poder y organización educacional: el caso peruano. *Aportes* 16, 92–111. Also in English version: 1971, Sociocultural constraints on Peruvian educational development. *Journal of Developing Areas* 5, 3, 401–15.
Peru, El Gubierno Revolucionario de la Fuerza Armada 1972, Ley General de Educación, Decreto 19326.
Peru, Ministerio de Educación 1972, Primer Seminario Nacional de Educación Bilingue: Algunos estudios y ponencias.
RUBIN, J. 1973, Language planning: discussion of some current issues. In J. RUBIN and R. SHUY (eds) *Language Planning: Current Issues and Research*. Washington, DC: Georgetown University Press.
RUBIN, J. and JERNUDD, B. J. (eds) 1971, *Can Language be Planned?* Honolulu: University of Hawaii, East–West Center.
STEIN, W. 1972, *Mestizo Cultural Patterns: Culture and Social Structure in the Peruvian Andes*. Buffalo, NY: New York State University Press.

Index